THE FIRST-YEAR
Seminar

Designing, Implementing, and Assessing Courses to Support Student Learning and Success

Using Peers in the Classroom

Volume Four

Jennifer A. Latino
and Michelle L. Ashcraft

NATIONAL RESOURCE CENTER
FIRST-YEAR EXPERIENCE® AND STUDENTS IN TRANSITION
UNIVERSITY OF SOUTH CAROLINA

Cite as:

Latino, J. A., & Ashcraft, M. L. (2012). *The first-year seminar: Designing, implementing, and assessing courses to support student learning and success: Vol. IV. Using peers in the classroom*. Columbia, SC: University of South Carolina, National Resource Center for The First-Year Experience and Students in Transition.

Production Staff for the National Resource Center:

Series Editor	Tracy L. Skipper, Assistant Director for Publications
Design and Production	Josh Tyler, Graphic Artist

Library of Congress Cataloging-in-Publication Data
Keup, Jennifer R.
 The first-year seminar : designing, implementing, and assessing courses to support student learning & success / Jennifer R. Keup and Joni Webb Petschauer.
    p. cm.
 Includes bibliographical references.
 ISBN 978-1-889271-79-8
 1. College freshmen--United States. 2. College student orientation--United States. 3. Interdisciplinary approach in education--United States. I. Petschauer, Joni Webb. II. Title.
 LB2343.32.K48 2011
 378.1'98--dc22
                    2011015354

Contents

List of Tables and Figures

Notes on the Series

The previous two volumes in this series have focused on instruction in the first-year seminar, with volume II outlining faculty training and development and volume III describing teaching strategies. Here, Jennifer Latino and Michelle Ashcraft continue this exploration by discussing the role of peers in seminar instruction. At the University of South Carolina—the birthplace of the modern first-year seminar—peer leaders have been a part of the instructional team for University 101 since 1993, and in recent years, every section of the course has had either an undergraduate or graduate student serving as a co-instructor. Yet, the use of undergraduate students in the instruction of first-year seminars nationally remains low, ranging from about 5% (Padgett & Keup, 2011) to about 25% (Barefoot, 2002). The purpose of this volume is, therefore, two-fold: (a) to help build a case for the value of using peers in the first-year seminar and (b) to provide insight on how to do so effectively.

Research on peer-to-peer mentoring suggests a number of positive academic and social outcomes for the students served. For example, Supplemental Instruction and other peer-led instructional models (e.g., Lewis & Lewis, 2005; Stone & Jacobs, 2008) have been linked to improved content mastery, higher course grades, and fewer course withdrawals. In other studies, peer interactions have correlated with increased retention (Switzer & Thomas, 1998) and academic success (Kim, 2009; Smith & Zhang, 2010) for underrepresented student populations. Additional positive outcomes for first-year students having peer mentoring experiences include increased engagement (Black & Voelker, 2008), satisfaction (Rose, 2003; Schrodt, Cawyer, & Sanders, 2003; Wasburn, 2008), sense of support (Reid, 2008; Colvin & Ashman, 2010; Yazedjian, Purswell, Toews, & Sevin, 2007), and improved academic skills (Landrum & Nelson, 2002). Colvin and Ashman (2010) found that students in a first-year seminar valued peer mentors for assisting them with course work, connecting them to the institution, helping them get involved on campus, and providing individual attention.

Yet, peer education experiences also facilitate important academic, social, and personal outcomes for the students who serve as mentors, including factual knowledge, helping others, friendships, personal growth, positive regard for the instructor, skills, and decision making (Badura, Miller, Johnson, Stewart, & Bartolomei, 2003). Students participating in a 2009 study noted improvements in interpersonal communication, organization, time management, presentation skills, understanding of diverse others, written communication, and academic skills as a result of peer leader experiences (National Resource Center, 2009). There is also evidence that serving as a peer leader may enhance institutional engagement, as students in this study reported more meaningful interactions with faculty, staff, and other students and a greater sense of belonging at the institution. In a more recent study (Colvin & Ashman, 2010), first-year seminar peer leaders identified "being able to support students, reapply[ing] concepts in their own lives, and developing connections themselves" as benefits of their experiences (p. 127).

Thus, the research on student success programs would seem to provide ample evidence that peer education benefits not only the students served but also the students offering academic and social support. Moreover, including peers as part of the first-year seminar instructional team would seem to increase the likelihood these courses would achieve their most frequently reported objectives: (a) developing academic skills, (b) creating a connection with the institution, and (c) providing an orientation to campus resources and service (Padgett & Keup, 2011).

As the evidence surrounding the benefits of peer education grows, we would hope to find peers as fixtures in first-year seminars at colleges and universities across the country. For program directors who are ready to make this transition, Latino and Ashcraft offer guidance in defining the roles peers can play in the course and in recruiting and selecting a strong group of student leaders. They also describe strategies for training and providing ongoing support to peers, paying particular attention to helping peers build effective relationships with their co-instructors.

While the research on peer education is compelling, it is nonetheless limited. There is still much we need to know about the outcomes students and their peer leaders experience and about which aspects of the experience may contribute to those outcomes. In this regard, well-designed program assessment and evaluation are essential for informing institutional-level practice and improving our understanding of peer mentoring. To this end, the authors conclude the volume with what can best be described as a 360-degree examination of the impact of peer instructors on the first-year seminar. This discussion offers a useful framework for creating an assessment plan for the peer instructor component of a first-year seminar.

We hope this volume offers readers both the rationale for designing an instructional model for the first-year seminar that includes undergraduate students and the tools to create or refine such a model. As you consider the strategies described here and examine them in light of your own practice, we invite your feedback on this work.

Tracy L. Skipper
Series Editor
National Resource Center for The First-Year Experience and
Students in Transition
University of South Carolina

Overview

Research surrounding peer education shows students can and do have significant positive impacts on the development and learning of their peers. As early as 1968, the Committee on the Student in Higher Education (Hazen Foundation) reported that the most effective teachers on a college campus were other students. Chickering (1969) echoed these findings with his report that peer groups were primary forces influencing college student development. Research over the past 40 years (Astin, 1993; Cuseo, 1991; Ender & Newton, 2000; Terenzini, Pascarella, & Blimling, 1996) has continued to support the idea that peer educators are an effective resource in programs designed to enhance student learning. Astin (1993) concluded "the student's peer group is the single most potent source of influence on growth and development during the undergraduate years" (p. 398). In particular, he suggested "students' values, beliefs, and aspirations tend to change in the direction of the dominant values, beliefs, and aspirations of the peer group," including political orientation and social activation and attitudes toward cultural awareness and diversity (Astin, 1993, p. 398).

Given its potential for shaping student learning and development, peer education is growing in many areas across campus, including residence life, admissions, health education, and academic support. The use of peers in the recruitment and orientation processes is especially common, with students serving as telecounselors and/or tour guides for prospective students. This interaction with current students provides prospective students with an honest perspective of what it means to be a student at a given institution. Peer-to-peer engagement continues through the orientation process, where older students are specifically trained to assist with the various responsibilities associated with hosting and acclimating new students to campus. Usually taken in the first semester of enrollment, first-year seminars are an extension of the orientation process and provide a space for students to share their challenges and learn from their peers facing similar transitions (Hunter & Linder, 2005). Thus, it would seem reasonable to continue using peer educators throughout the orientation process, including the first-year seminar. Yet, there is much room for growth in peer educator involvement in seminars. The 2009 National Survey of First-Year Seminars (Padgett & Keup, 2011), for example, found that only 5% of institutions with first-year seminars used undergraduates as part of the instructional team. As such, this volume provides rationale for and methods to support a peer education component in the first-year seminar.

What Is a Peer Educator?

Peers are used to assist students in a variety of ways on campuses across the United States and internationally. To some extent, the definition of a peer educator is contingent on the role the student plays. In an effort to gauge the breadth of peer education on college and university campuses, the National Resource Center for The First-Year Experience and Students in Transition conducted a national survey of peer leadership in spring 2009 (Keup & Skipper, 2010). Respondents reported involvement in peer education programs hosted by athletics, academics, community service, counseling or mental health, judicial affairs, multicultural affairs, orientation, physical health and wellness, religious organizations, residence life, student government, student productions, and study abroad programs. Students were also likely to have held a range of peer educator roles. More than half reported holding between two and four positions throughout their college experience. Academic programs were the most commonly reported sponsors of peer leader experiences, with 58.6% of survey respondents indicating involvement in such a program. Titles for academic peer leader roles included first-year seminar leader, tutor, academic mentor, peer advisor, and teaching assistant (Keup & Skipper, 2010). Throughout the volume, we examine the responses of academic leaders to learn more about the peer educator experience.

This focus on academic support roles in some ways mirrors the definition presented by Newton and Ender (2010), who describe peer educators as "students who have been selected, trained, and designated by a campus authority to offer educational services to their peers. These services are intentionally designed to assist peers toward attainment of educational goals" (p. 6). Using Newton and Ender's definition as a framework, this volume assumes peer educators play an instructional role (i.e., helping plan the syllabus and selected activities or assignments, facilitating classroom activities, providing course-related assistance to enrolled students) in the first-year seminar. While the emphasis here is on the educative function, the terms *peer educator, peer leader*, and *peer mentor* will be used interchangeably throughout this volume since they reflect the range of terms colleges and universities have used to refer to an upper-division student who has been selected to help a full-time faculty or staff member plan and facilitate a first-year seminar. Many components of peer education have universal application, regardless of hosting department, title, or position description. Thus, educators from a range of departments, programs, and disciplines are likely to find the information presented in this volume useful and applicable to their programs.

Organization of the Volume

Chapter 1 serves as an overview of the various roles and responsibilities of the peer leader. Through the lens of the 4 Cs (i.e., companion, connector, coach, and champion), the expectations of peer leaders for the first-year seminar are presented. Program developers will be prompted to consider the expectations they have for peer leaders. Readers will also find practical methods for building the relationship between peer leaders and faculty, and peer leaders and first-year students.

In chapter 2, we look to the benefits of connecting peer education to the seminar. Because the focus in the literature tends to be on the benefits that accrue to the students served, we place special emphasis on the learning and development that occurs for students engaged in the peer leadership role. The chapter begins with an exploration of the educational context of the seminar and the potential impact on the peer leader's attitude toward learning, academic motivations, and behavior. We also explore a range of outcomes related to the peer leadership experience, including transferrable career skills, academic skills, and interpersonal skills. The chapter closes with a discussion of strategies for supporting peer educator development through assessment and training.

Chapter 3 provides practical and easy-to-apply processes and procedures for recruiting and selecting peer leaders. Readers will be prompted to reflect on the profile of an ideal peer educator given the parameters of their course and institution. Once the position description is refined, program directors can begin the process of recruiting and selecting peer educators. The chapter offers a framework for developing an application and describes strategies for marketing the position and selecting a cohort of peer leaders. Chapter 3 also takes up the ever-important question of how peer educators should be compensated.

Chapter 4 provides a rationale for the importance of training programs designed to build skills and confidence in peer leaders, including the development of learning outcomes and use of assessment results to shape training content and processes. Intentional training efforts help distinguish students as educators rather than mere influencers of their peers. The chapter will also provide strategies for developing successful ongoing development programs and examples of agendas for one-day and semester-long training experiences.

Chapter 5 identifies the various constituents who benefit from a peer education program (i.e., first-year learners, peer educators, and first-year seminar programs) and recommends assessment and evaluation efforts that measure the impact on each of these groups. Program evaluation should serve not as the end point for a peer leadership program but rather the cornerstone when developing or rejuvenating a program. Effective evaluation can help program personnel justify the resources that are dedicated to peer leadership programs and should also drive decisions about the future of the program, including defining peer roles and responsibilities, selecting staff, and developing training initiatives.

Additional Resources

Throughout the text are examples of materials used by various campuses. These samples are provided to assist readers in creating new programs and rejuvenating or sustaining existing programs. To help program leaders gain a better understanding of the theory and research undergirding peer education, a bibliography is included in appendix A. The resources listed touch on a broad range of peer education roles both within and beyond the first-year seminar. Program administrators may find it valuable to review the literature on different peer education roles to gain diverse perspectives on recruiting, training, developing, supporting, and evaluating peer educators. Other appendices in the volume offer models for building peer-instructor relationships, training peer leaders, and evaluating the peer leader experience.

This volume, written by professionals whose work is heavily focused on administering programs and supporting students who are helping other students, was developed to provide a blend of the theoretical basis for peer leadership within the first-year seminar and the practical applications of our work. Readers will find this publication useful whether considering the implementation of a new peer leadership program or seeking to improve an existing program.

Chapter 1
Peer Roles and Responsibilities in the First-Year Seminar

The classroom is like the stage or the screen on which the instructor plays the lead, performing day after day for the sake of the audience's learning. Those who admire performance and film know that rarely can a single actor be successful in portraying an entire story; rather, it is the interactions with and support from other cast members that truly engage the audience. Therefore, if the instructor is the lead, then a peer educator could serve as the best supporting actor in facilitating the first-year seminar. For peer educators to be successful in this role, they must understand the expectations for their position, their various responsibilities in supporting first-year students inside and outside the classroom, and strategies for developing both professional partnerships and personal relationships with their co-instructors.

In serving as the best supporting actor, the peer educator supports both the instructor (lead) and the class (audience). That assistance should not be taken for granted by course coordinators and instructors, as considerable research has shown most facets of college student development are affected by peer influence (Antonio, 2004; Astin, 1993; Buote, 2006; Feldman & Newcomb, 1969; Kuh, Kinzie, Schuh, & Whitt, 2005; Pascarella & Terenzini, 1991; Swenson, Nordstrom, & Hiester, 2008), particularly students' commitment of the time and energy needed to succeed academically (Coleman, 1961; Cuseo, 2010a; Griffin & Romm, 2008; McDill & Rigsby, 1973; Wyckoff, 1999). Often students who elect to serve as peer educators indicate they did not fully understand the importance of the first-year seminar curriculum as a first-year student. They only began to appreciate the course as they moved on in their collegiate career and were forced to use some of the lessons and skills taught in the course. Many wish they had paid more attention at the time.

While the instructor can deliver material on seminar topics (e.g., effective time management and study skills, the importance of getting involved on campus, and how to use academic resources), it is likely the material will appear more relevant to the students if the peer educator can share personal experiences that persuade them to pay attention and take the information seriously. Therefore, the primary expectation for peer educators in the classroom is to positively influence the students in taking advantage of the course. To that end, this chapter examines four common roles peers take on with respect to students served and identifies strategies for negotiating those roles. Because the relationship between the instructor and the peer is also critical to the success of the course, the chapter concludes by examining strategies for building strong instructor-peer relationships.

Developing Peer-to-Peer Relationships

Much work has been done to define the roles of students who will work with other students as educators, mentors, advisors, student assistants, ambassadors, tutors, orientation leaders, resident assistants, or in some other peer-to-peer-serving capacity (Cuseo, 2010a; Ender & Newton, 2000; Hamid, 2001; Newton & Ender, 2010; Rice & Brown, 1990; Sanft, Jensen, & McMurray, 2008). Yet, the roles peer educators will hold and the expectations for their participation in the classroom will vary from campus to campus, program to program, and class to class depending on the curriculum, goals, and learning outcomes for the course; the individual goals of the instructors and peer leaders; and the combined personalities of the teaching team. Despite the individual differences in the peer educator experience, most program coordinators will define a set of core roles and responsibilities for peer leaders, especially those related to forming relationships with the students served. These can be summarized as the 4 Cs of peer education: (a) companion, (b) connector, (c) coach, and (d) champion.

The Companion Role

Passing out index cards on the first day of class in a first-year seminar and asking students to answer the following questions can lead to a list of varied answers touching on academic success and campus involvement issues: What are three reasons you took this class? What are three things you hope to get out of this class? and What do you hope to accomplish in your first semester and first year on campus? One issue that will be listed consistently among many students each semester will be their desire to make friends (Smith & Wertlieb, 2005; Weissberg, Owen, Jenkins, & Harburg, 2003). In fact, students expect to make new friends from diverse groups, and their satisfaction with college may depend on feeling connected to peers on campus (Larose & Boivin, 1998; Paul & Brier, 2001; Smith & Wertlieb, 2005; Weissberg et al., 2003). The students' priority for making friends may be explained in part by student development and human motivational theory. For example, Chickering and Reisser (1993) indicate the development of mature interpersonal relationships (i.e., companions) contributes to students' identity development at an earlier point than do academic, career, and life goals (i.e., developing purpose). Schlossberg, Waters, and Goodman (1995) note the importance of support (i.e., friends) in helping students cope with common transitional issues. Finally, Maslow's (1954) work suggests students must fulfill social (i.e., companionship) needs before they can fulfill any sort of higher-order needs, such as esteem and self-actualization. Thus, one of the most important roles for peer educators is that of a companion, who supports new students and facilitates the development of friendships with classmates and other peers.

Developing trusted friendships with the students is arguably the most important task for peer educators, as students will be more likely to view them as connectors, coaches, and champions once companionship is established. In order to fulfill the companion role peer educators may take on some or all of responsibilities described below.

Learning students' names. The first step in making a friend is meeting the person and learning his or her name. Being able to address students by name as quickly as possible will make facilitating friendships with the students much easier for the peer educator. Learning names is also important since first-year students will often seek out the peer educator before approaching the instructor, and peer educators need to be able to acknowledge the student and report back to the instructor on the issue discussed. Peer educators can be in charge of three tasks to assist them in learning students' names:

» **Name tents.** Either prior to or on the first day of class, the peer educator should make sure each student has a name tent. The peer educator should be responsible for collecting these at the end of each class and redistributing them at the beginning of each new session. Doing so will not only allow the peer educator and instructor to learn names but will help students learn one another's names as well.

» **Flash cards and cheat sheets.** On the first day of class, the peer educator should consider taking a picture of each student holding his or her name tent. These pictures can be printed individually as flash cards or imported into a cheat sheet to assist the peer educator and instructor in learning students' names.

» **Attendance.** Many instructors view taking attendance as a mundane task, but one that is nonetheless important. Putting the peer educator in charge of this task will enable him or her to learn the names of the students more quickly.

Making the digital connection early. Today's incoming students have grown up in the digital age. They form relationships online and may be more likely to text a question than to raise their hands and ask it in class. As today's peer educators have also grown up in the digital age and may be more familiar with the latest technology than the instructors with whom they are paired, they can use technology to communicate effectively and build relationships with and between the students. Two tools peer educators can use to make the digital connection include

» **Cell phones.** Most peer educators will feel comfortable giving their cell phone number to the students in their classes, and these numbers (i.e., both the peer educator's and students') should be exchanged during introductions on the first day of class. That way, if the students have questions outside of class, they can easily call or text the peer educator. In addition, an occasional text message from the peer educator to a student just to check in, ask how an exam went, or see how the weekend was can go a long way in developing relationships with students.

» **Facebook groups.** It is likely most incoming students and peer educators have Facebook accounts, and these students are used to interacting on the social network daily to keep up with friends, find out information, and meet new people. Many students have access to smart phones that allow them to keep up with Facebook throughout the day, so it can be a much faster way to communicate with students than e-mail. While some students may feel uncomfortable interacting with faculty, staff, and other authority figures on Facebook, they are very comfortable interacting with other students. Peer educators who set up a group for their class will find they can use the group as an easy way to send announcements to students, answer questions through Facebook's chat and messaging functions, and facilitate connections between the students using the group's message boards.

Planning and facilitating icebreakers. Whatever one's personal opinion about icebreakers may be, they are effective in getting students to learn each other's names and find commonalities. Encouraging and allowing peer educators to plan and facilitate icebreakers at the beginning of each class (at least for the first few sessions) can have an immense impact on building community among the students and with the instructor team. Peer educators should keep the following in mind when preparing and executing icebreakers:

» **Using name games or incorporating names in the icebreaker.** Doing so will help all parties—students, peer educators, and instructors—learn one another's names as quickly as possible.

» **Getting students up and moving around.** In most classes, students spend the majority of their time sitting in a chair either listening to an instructor or working in groups. Getting the students up and moving around will energize them and encourage them to get to know students other than those sitting closest to them.

» **Encouraging students to get to know everyone in class.** Peer educators should facilitate icebreakers so students interact with different people over the course of the term. By counting them off in teams, dividing the group according to different characteristics, or rotating students through activities, peer educators can ensure all students get to know all other students in class.

» **Participating in the activity.** Too often, peer educators will lead the students in icebreakers without actually participating themselves or encouraging the instructors to participate. This can result in students learning names and finding commonalities with one another while the peer educators and instructors do not. By participating, peer educators will more quickly develop a companionship with the students. Further, instructor participation allows the peer educator to facilitate the students getting to know the instructor personally, rather than just as a lecturer or authority figure.

Meeting with students individually outside of class. Depending on the time commitment programs require of their peer educators, individual conferences may be promoted as an optional expectation. Meeting individually with first-year students can enhance the relationship between the students and the peer educators and help the first-year students feel an enhanced sense of community within the class. An informal get-together outside of class in a comfortable space allows the peer educators to more easily develop a friendship with each student. This act temporarily removes the authority from the peer educators and exchanges the academic environment of the classroom for the social environment of the campus coffee shop, study lounge, or student union patio. Once the students feel more connected to the peer educators socially, they will be more likely to interact with them in class. Holding at least one of these meetings at the beginning of the semester will allow the peer educators to be more informed of each students' interests and goals and become better connectors, coaches, champions, and captains throughout the rest of the term.

The Connector Role

College offers a unique opportunity for students to meet new people, get involved in new activities, discover new interests, and take advantage of a newfound responsibility for learning in many situations and venues, both inside and outside the classroom. However, finding ways to do all of this can be both challenging and overwhelming for students, many of whom are far from home and on their own for the first time. These challenges and feelings of being overwhelmed are exacerbated by unfamiliarity with the physical campus layout, the bureaucratic structure of the institution, and complicated terminology littered with acronyms and university-specific slang. Retention research (Astin, 1999; Ishler & Upcraft, 2005; Tinto, 1993; Tinto & Pusser, 2006; Upcraft & Gardner, 1989) indicates universities have a relatively short window of time to help students gain familiarity with resources; get connected with campus activities; learn the language; and develop relationships with peers, faculty, and staff in order to keep students enrolled and on a path toward graduation. Further, lack of fit (specifically, unmet expectations) impacts students' performance and success (Smith & Wertlieb, 2005; Weissberg, et al., 2003) and may ultimately result in their departure from the institution. As experienced students who have learned the campus language and how to navigate campus academically and socially, peer educators play a vital role in helping new students make connections to their new educational home and community.

Many peer educators assume their role because they want to help other students. Often in interviews and focus groups, many will discuss how they formed a connection with someone on campus—a staff member, a faculty member, a friend, an upper-division student mentor—who helped them navigate the campus, allowing them to effectively use campus resources and take advantage of the opportunities to get involved both inside and outside the classroom. These student leaders essentially want to pay it forward by helping new students in the ways someone else helped them. Others will indicate how they felt lost in their first year on campus attempting to learn about resources, activities, and requirements. These students want to assist new students in order to prevent them from feeling as lost as they did. Whatever their reasons for assuming the role, the peer educators' personal experiences will motivate them to both help connect the new students to campus and feel more comfortable in working through these common transitional issues.

On large and small campuses, disseminating information is a preeminent concern for the institution, and awareness of information is a major challenge for students. Students, especially those who are new to campus, can be easily confused and overwhelmed by a constant barrage of posters, e-mails, social networking posts and messages, flyers, mail, phone calls and text messages, banners, t-shirts, and many other avenues that campus constituencies use to promote services, events, course requirements, and programs. Yet, despite the constant stream of information, many students, if asked, would likely not be able restate the majority of messages. There is simply too much information to sift through. Thus, it becomes the responsibility of the peer educator to not only be aware of a multitude of campus policies, resources, announcements, and activities, but also to sort through it all and present the most relevant information to first-year students. To do that and most effectively fulfill the connector role, peer educators may assume the responsibilities described below.

Making sense of the alphabet soup. While today's students are accustomed to texting and social networking language that is littered with acronyms, coming to college can make them feel like they are swimming in a bowl of alphabet soup. When every campus building, college major or program, department, resource, and activity is shortened to an acronym, navigating the university can be overwhelming for even the most text-savvy student. Add in the campus slang, and the average student can feel like he or she has landed in a foreign country rather than on college campus. Therefore, high on the priority list and one of the easiest ways to make students feel connected to campus is to teach them the language. When peer educators refer to buildings, majors, programs, departments, and services on campus, they should indicate both the acronym and what it stands for. They should also be cognizant of campus slang and explain such terms when they are used in class. This can be accomplished in both daily conversation and in fun activities, such as a campus lingo quiz or *Jeopardy* game. New students will feel much more a part of campus when they know *A&S* indicates classes in the arts and sciences, *the lawn* refers to the most popular green space on campus, and *grabbing JJ's* means getting a sub from the popular off-campus sandwich shop.

Giving students a campus tour. Peer educators can calm many fears by teaching students how to navigate the physical campus (e.g., personally conducting a tour, explaining a campus map in class). When asked what they are most nervous about on the first day of class, new students often place "making it to class on time" or "finding my classes" at the top of the list. Peer educators who know the building codes, the layout of the classrooms in the most common buildings, the university transportation options and bus routes, and the most convenient routes or hidden shortcuts between buildings can best show students how to find their classrooms and make it to them on time.

Developing a campus scavenger hunt as a class activity. Finding classes and the best routes between them is just the first step in learning to navigate campus. Students also need to know how to find resources, common departments, and popular recreational spaces on campus. Peer educators can be very helpful in developing a list of popular hangouts, the best places to eat, secret study spots, and unique campus landmarks. By adding locations of important offices and resources to this list, peer educators can create a scavenger hunt that will be fun and educational. New students can participate in teams during class time to complete the scavenger hunt. This will allow them to get to know their classmates while also learning how to navigate the campus and locate important resources and departments that can assist them during their collegiate careers.

Explaining and reviewing campus resources. Many instructors will provide students with a list of campus resources attached to the course syllabus. This is certainly helpful as a reference tool, but discussing and promoting these resources in class will better encourage students to use them. Peer educators can take a few moments at the end of each class period to discuss a campus resource related to the day's topic or what the students are experiencing at that point in the semester. For example, they can discuss using the campus writing center before midterms, or promote the institution's peer tutoring program after talking about effective study strategies in class. Additionally, when possible, the peer educator should share personal experiences using the resource(s) to demonstrate it is appropriate to seek assistance when needed.

Making regular announcements. New students need to be educated on and reminded of important campus deadlines, such as when tuition bills or scholarship applications are due and when course registration for the next semester occurs. They should also be told about cocurricular opportunities on campus (e.g., leadership, study abroad, and student employment) as well as respective deadlines for getting involved. Peer educators who remain familiar with the campus calendar and stay informed of opportunities on campus can make daily announcements to best inform the students in their classes.

Encouraging students to get involved on campus. One of the characteristics most common to those students who are retained by campuses is that they are involved in some sort of activity or leadership role on campus (Astin, 1999; Pascarella & Terenzini, 1991, 2005). Peer educators are likely engaged in other roles and activities on campus beyond coteaching the first-year seminar, and may have friends who are involved, too. Whether attending campus activities and student organization meetings is part of the course's curriculum or not, peer educators should promote ways to get involved on campus, including how to find out about student organizations and apply for student leadership opportunities.

The Coach Role

Just as an athletic coach's role is to teach players how to succeed in a sport, the first-year seminar instructional team's role is to teach students how to succeed in college—academically and socially—and develop skills that will help them succeed far beyond the collegiate years. Depending on the institution, the program, and the teaching team, peer educators may teach entire lessons, coteach others, or have no teaching responsibilities. Regardless of who presents a lesson, the peer educator can play a vital role in providing an experienced student's perspective on the topic; demonstrating its importance in student success; and facilitating discussion pertaining to any associated issues, questions, and concerns.

In addition to wanting to help other students, many peer educators are also interested in developing presentation and facilitation skills that will further their success in college and beyond. They come into the role with a desire to help implement and facilitate the curriculum, and they often provide a unique perspective that can increase the interest in and retention of important topics relevant to the first-year transition.

Teaching and facilitating lessons in which peers may have a greater influence. No matter how young, cool, up-to-speed with the current students' culture, nice, relatable, wise, or interested in impacting students' lives an instructor is, peers will often have more credibility with certain topics (e.g., those related to the college social scene, behavior, and lifestyle). Students may be more likely to listen to a peer educator talk about getting involved on campus, building a campus network, making responsible decisions surrounding sexual health or alcohol use, managing money, or seeking campus employment or internships because they recognize the peer educator is dealing with these issues on the same campus and at the same time. While instructors may have similarly valuable lessons and opinions to share about these topics, students may perceive them as too far removed from their experience to see the instructors' views as valid. Peer educators can also be influential in delivering academic-related content, particularly lessons related to skills development. For example, a peer educator can demonstrate the importance of time management or good note-taking skills by showing students his or her personal planner or reworked class notes.

Peer educators should also be used to provide real-life examples to which students can relate. Program coordinators and/or instructors may also consider requiring particular lessons be taught by peer educators, both to have the most influence on the new students and to ensure the peer educators are getting the most out of their experience. For instance, the University of Kentucky requires their peer instructors to teach the lessons on note taking, alcohol use, bystander intervention, and career development, though most also play a role in facilitating the academic expectations, library, diversity, common reading, and campus involvement sessions.

Modeling appropriate behavior. If peer educators are going to play a role in teaching new students how to be successful, they need to follow their own advice and model good behaviors. It would be difficult for new students to understand the importance of attending and participating in class if the peer educator was regularly late and sat in the back of the classroom reading the newspaper. It would also be hard for students to develop appropriate habits for alcohol use if the peer leader was observed abusing alcohol at a weekend party. However, it is not realistic to expect peer educators to be perfect students. In some cases, they can successfully influence students by admitting mistakes and suggesting what they have learned from them. Therefore, peer educators should take note of the curriculum prior to the start of the semester and determine where they can most effectively share their experiences to support the lessons.

The Champion Role

Many new students come to college having had a host of people in their lives—parents, family members, teachers, high school counselors, coaches, and peers—looking out for their best interests. Leading up to enrollment in college, these same individuals may have guided students toward activities and resources that would ultimately ensure their successful admission to college. Once on campus, however, many students may feel they are a single drop in a sea of students who are all trying to find their way on their own, and many are in search of someone who can hold them accountable and point them in the right direction when necessary. The peer educator can serve as a champion for these students by advocating on their behalf, or teaching them how to advocate for themselves, and by connecting them to various people in the campus network when additional assistance is needed.

To be a champion for the new students in their classes, peer educators must be aware of students' rights and responsibilities. They must also be able to recognize when students need additional support and know where to send them for assistance. Peer educators can be a champion for students in the some of the ways described below.

Personally introducing students to campus resources. As peer educators notice students in need of various campus resources, they need to remind them of the options available. However, peer educators will often find that many new students are intimated to walk into the campus counseling center, tutoring center, financial aid office, or any other office with which they are unfamiliar. When possible, peer educators should offer to take the students personally to the appropriate staff member or service they need. New students may be more willing to seek assistance if they do not have to face asking for help alone.

Helping students become involved on campus. As is the case with seeking out campus resources, new students may find it intimidating to attend a student organization meeting or pursue a campus leadership opportunity. Peer educators can champion students' desires to become involved by volunteering to go with them to a student organization meeting or event for the first time. Additionally, as peer educators recognize potential in their students, they can encourage them to get involved by talking about leadership opportunities and personally forwarding applications. Students may be more interested in applying and feel they will be successful if a peer educator tells them they have potential. To advocate for students' involvement, the peer educator can serve as a reference, when possible, or encourage the instructor to serve as a reference.

Developing Professional and Personal Co-Instructor Relationships

In selection interviews, peer educators commonly cite two reasons for wanting to take on such a leadership role. First, as noted previously, they want to help new students make a successful transition to college. Beyond that, they also want to build a relationship with the faculty or staff members with whom they will be paired to coteach. These students anticipate and desire close relationships with professors and staff much like the relationships they had with high school teachers, guidance counselors, and coaches. Research (Astin, 1999) also indicates developing and maintaining such desired relationships with faculty is important to student success and retention:

> Frequent interaction with faculty is more strongly related to satisfaction with college than any other type of involvement or, indeed, any other student or institutional characteristic. Students who interact frequently with faculty members are more likely than other students to express satisfaction with all aspects of their institutional experience, including student friendships, variety of courses, intellectual environment, and even the administration of the institution. Thus, finding ways to encourage greater student involvement with faculty (and vice versa) could be a highly productive activity on most college campuses. (p. 525)

Therefore, developing peer educator-instructor teaching teams not only benefits the first-year seminar program and the first-year students who enroll, but also ensures the peer educators' satisfaction, success, and retention.

However, the relationship the peer educator will form with his or her co-instructor is unique and likely different from any relationship the peer has had with teachers, counselors, coaches, and other professionals in the past. By taking on the peer leader role, students enter into a dichotomous relationship with their co-instructor, one in which they are both a mentee and a peer. As such, defining roles and setting expectations pertaining to this relationship are critically important to effective teaching teams. While the specific roles and expectations for peer leaders and instructors will vary depending on their personalities, course administrators can present general expectations for the relationship, a list of roles that need to be filled, and a list of tasks the team should accomplish. Course administrators can use training and development sessions to help teams define their working relationships.

Setting Expectations for the Peer Educator-Instructor Team

After completing their individual application, acceptance, and training processes, peer educators and instructors should generally understand their individual roles and the expectations for team teaching the first-year seminar. However, to further explain, develop, and encourage these partnerships, a joint conversation with peer educators and instructors should articulate detailed expectations, as well as recommendations for developing appropriate relationships and for effectively team teaching the course. Doing so can help course administrators prevent confusion by ensuring both peer educators and instructors have heard the same information. Setting these expectations also increases accountability for instructors who are not experienced in team teaching or who may be reluctant to accept the peer educator as a cofacilitator by demonstrating how to share responsibilities effectively. Finally, such discussions might encourage peer educators who may be shy about articulating their desires to be involved in the course to volunteer for specific responsibilities.

Programs may focus on teaching team development in different venues, such as a matching session, team-teaching session, or planning workshop. The opportunity allows teaching teams to learn more about roles and expectations and peer educators to meet their co-instructors, as well as spend time working together to define their relationship. An example agenda for a workshop of this kind is found in appendix B.

Defining Roles and Responsibilities

In defining the roles and responsibilities of the teaching teams and setting expectations for their relationship, it is appropriate for program administrators to speak individually to each constituent group as well as to everyone collectively. For example, program administrators would address the peer educators about the role of their instructors, address the instructors about the role of the peer educators, and address everyone about expectations for their partnerships.

Instructors' responsibilities. Instructors and peer educators should expect the following in terms of instructors' roles and responsibilities in the classroom, as well as their obligations to the peer educators:

» **Engaging the peer educator in developing and/or giving feedback on lessons plans.** Involving the peer educator in course planning will keep the lessons fresh and student-focused. It will also allow peer educators to apply their knowledge of active-learning pedagogy from training.

» **Allowing peer educators to teach the lessons they are assigned to teach.** Whether dictated by courses administrators or agreed upon by through individual conversations within the teaching team, a plan should be in place outlining specific teaching responsibilities for the peer leader. Overriding the course administrators or reneging on agreements and not allowing peer educators to teach assigned lessons may result in them feeling unfulfilled in their role or as though their time spent in training has been wasted.

» **Encouraging and supporting peer educators' further involvement.** Supporting peer educators' personal initiative and choice in their roles and responsibilities will lead to improved intrinsic motivation (Wellman, 2008), increasing their likelihood of success in the seminar program.

» **Asking peer educators to provide real-life examples.** Even when instructors are leading lessons in class, they should engage peer educators in providing examples from a student perspective on how the information can be applied or used for learning and success.

» **Providing ongoing feedback.** Instructors should take responsibility for developing peer educators' skills. Both positive feedback and constructive criticism needs to be given each time peer educators lead a lesson or activity to enhance their presentation, facilitation, and communication skills. Instructors should also share course evaluations with the peer educator.

» **Assigning grades.** While peer educators may give feedback on assignments, authority for grading should remain with the instructor so as to prevent peer educators from having to evaluate other students (some of whom may become friends) and navigate potential grade disputes.

Peer educators' responsibilities. Peer educators and instructors should expect the following in terms of peer educators' roles and responsibilities in the classroom and in terms of their obligations to the instructors:

» **Engaging in class.** Even when not leading the lesson, peer educators can be a reality check for new students by providing real-life examples that support what the instructor is teaching.
» **Keeping the instructor informed.** As students will often come to the peer educator first with personal issues and questions, the peer educator should commit to keeping the instructor informed of issues that may impact the students' success.
» **Voicing opinions, taking initiative, and communicating needs.** Peer educators need to communicate to instructors if they feel they are being asked to do too much or too little, if they have an idea for improving the lesson plan or course, or if they need additional support from the instructor.

Shared responsibilities. In order develop and maintain the most effective partnership, peer educators and instructors should commit to the following shared responsibilities:

» **Meeting regularly.** To plan effectively for class and develop a successful relationship with one another, peer educators and instructors should meet in person at least once a week.
» **Communicating effectively and in a timely fashion.** Peer educators and instructors should discuss their preferences for communicating with one another (i.e., phone, text message, e-mail, social networking) and commit to responding to messages in a timely manner.
» **Planning the syllabus together.** Both the peer educator and instructor should have input in the order of lessons, type of assignments, class policies, and planned activities. Additionally, both need to be aware of the syllabus in its entirety so they can answer student questions and fill in for the other as necessary.

» **Dividing and defining roles and responsibilities.** Prior to the start of the semester, peer educators and instructors should work together to decide who will be responsible for specific lessons, activities, and logistical tasks. A worksheet can be provided to both parties as a guideline (see appendix B). Kevesdy and Burich (1997) offered the following types of questions to help peers and instructors explore teaching responsibilities:

- How comfortable are we, individually and together, with the various course topics?
- Do we have the resources to cover every topic? If not, are there other experts or guest speakers who might be of assistance?
- How will we divide the tasks for class preparation (e.g., taking attendance, keeping grades, handing out papers, making copies, contacting guest speakers)?
- How will we divide teaching responsibilities?
- How will we present a united front to our students?

» **Supporting one another in the classroom.** Peer educators and instructors will disagree at times. However, discussion about these matters should be handled outside the classroom. Both should commit to maintaining a balanced relationship with the class, avoiding the good-cop-bad-cop scenario, in which the instructor is often seen as the disciplinarian while the peer educator is seen as the friend.

» **Accepting feedback and constructive criticism.** Both peer educators and instructors should be willing to share feedback and accept criticism, knowing such conversations are important for both personal and course improvements.

Developing Personal Relationships

In addition to working together for course-related purposes, it is expected, encouraged, and recommended that peer educators form personal relationships with instructors independent of their co-instructor partnership. Developing a relationship beyond the classroom as the co-instructors' mentee and friend can personally benefit both the peer educator and the instructor and can be integral to the success of the first-year seminar. The more comfortable peer educators and instructors are with each other outside the classroom, the more comfortable they will be coteaching inside the classroom. If students sense the peer educator is comfortable with the instructor, they may feel more at ease interacting with the instructor and in class in general. Strategies for helping co-instructors develop personal relationships include

» Meeting for a meal occasionally throughout the semester
» Celebrating birthdays, holidays, and major milestones (e.g., a good grade on an exam, receipt of an award, the end of the semester) together
» Spending a small portion of each weekly meeting catching up on each other's personal lives (e.g., school, work, family, friends)
» Staying in touch with instructors beyond the semester in which they coteach

Conclusion

Student leaders frequently choose to enlist in peer educator opportunities within the first-year seminar because they want to help new students make a successful transition and develop personal relationships with faculty and/ or staff members on campus. These desires serve as intrinsic motivation. However, for peer educators to be truly successful in supporting first-year students, they must understand the various roles they are expected to fulfill and the purpose of those roles. Additionally, as the co-instructor relationship is unique, peer educators must understand how to develop both professional and personal relationships with their co-instructors. Program administrators can set these expectations through the application, interview and selection process (chapter 3); explain and teach the roles through training (chapter 4); and facilitate role definition and relationship development through a collaborative working session for both peer educators and instructors.

Chapter 2
Foundations for Growth and Development in Peer Educators

Today's college students often view postsecondary education as an opportunity for self-exploration and holistic development rather than a collection of course credits assembled to earn a diploma. Students arrive on campus with the expectation that cocurricular experiences will supplement their in-class learning and make them more marketable to future employers. For example, students may see out-of-class experiences as an opportunity to gain important career skills, such as the top five qualities employers look for in college graduates—verbal communication skills, a strong work ethic, teamwork skills, analytical skills, and initiative (NACE, 2011). These skills can be presented and discussed in a classroom environment; however, opportunities for practice and application will better prepare students for the workforce and will help set them apart from their peers.

The focus of the peer educator program is frequently the learning, development, and success of the students served with little attention paid to the personal development peer leaders may experience by taking on this role. Yet, peer educators report that educating and mentoring their peers enhances their current skills and helps them develop new ones. Similarly, the National Clearinghouse of Leadership Programs at the University of Maryland reports that students experience significant growth in leadership when institutions develop programs that "foster leadership skills in students and effectively teach them to lead other students" (Adelman, 2002, p. 5). Other research suggests students serving in peer mentoring roles for first-year students experience growth "in areas related to identity and sense of purpose" (Harmon, 2006, p. 58). Through well-developed peer education programs, students can be expected to develop higher-level cognitive skills (Cuseo, 1991).

McDaniels et al. (1994) suggest that peer leadership roles provide a "theoretical base for the practical application of their skills" and that students in such roles "learn to take responsibility, [handle] a wide range of professional and ethical issues, and gain a sense of self-worth" (quoted in Adelman, 2002, p. 26). Additionally, peers may report gains in their confidence, personal responsibility, and academic achievement (McKinney & Reynolds, 2002).

When intentionally designed with both the first-year student's and the peer educator's development in mind, first-year seminars allow student leaders to explore their own skills while receiving support and encouragement from caring faculty and staff. This chapter will address the types of learning and development peer educators are likely to experience and describe strategies for designing programs to achieve these outcomes.

The Educational Context of First-Year Seminar Peer Leadership

Serving as a peer leader for a first-year seminar affords students a unique perspective on higher education. No longer strictly consumers of higher education, they now also play a role in the delivery of educational experiences to their fellow students. As they work with their co-instructors to plan their seminars, peer educators learn about course and syllabus design, pedagogy, and faculty expectations for student behavior. Exposure to such topics often prompts peer educators to reflect on, and perhaps reconsider, their own behavior in the classroom, their perceptions of and relationships with instructors, and their opinions of course content and teaching pedagogy. Peer educators can then influence the first-year students' attitudes and behaviors by providing insight into the instructor's perspective. Further, they may find themselves adopting more effective habits for and attitudes toward learning, making them a stronger role model for the new students they serve. To understand the learning and developmental outcomes peer leaders may experience, it is important to explore the educational context in which they find themselves.

Course and Syllabus Design

As noted in chapter 1, peer educators should take an active role in planning the course syllabus along with corresponding lesson plans, class activities, and assignments. Few, if any, peer educators will have previously had this experience. The initial observation for many peers engaged in this process is the amount of time and effort required, which can give them some insight into instructors' commitment to student learning, development, and success. Hopefully, peer educators will also begin to make connections between the first-year seminar goals and the activities and assignments included in the course. While peer educators' more recent experiences as first-year students can help inform the syllabus design, the task also provides a unique opportunity for critical thinking and reflection pertaining to the ideal order of topics and corresponding assignments, especially since nearly every seminar topic can be considered high priority for new students' successful transitions.

First-Year Seminar Pedagogy

Once the larger issues of course design are addressed, peer educators may engage in the development of individual lesson plans, especially if there is an expectation that they will teach partial or whole class sessions on their own. They experience first-hand the challenges associated with lesson plan development, including how long they take to create and how difficult it can be to formulate an active-learning environment. Students who understand the process of developing a college-level course are more likely to appreciate the work of faculty campuswide, making for a stronger relationship between students and faculty. In addition, this experience will challenge the peer educators to use creativity and critical thinking in designing active-learning opportunities for the students and will also evoke appreciation for how the courses they are enrolled in are executed.

As students, peer educators have likely felt frustrated with class projects, exams, and assignments, particularly if the purpose is unclear. However, in their role as peer educators, they are now partially responsible for student learning in the first-year seminar. In working with their co-instructor to develop assignments for the course, peer educators can gain a new perspective on the purpose of assignments, exams, and projects, especially when they are able to connect these to larger course goals or specific learning objectives. The process-oriented nature of the first-year seminar means peer leaders will likely be exposed to assignment design emphasizing analysis, synthesis, and application rather than simple recall and understanding. Participating in this kind of activity may not immediately change peer educators' attitudes about such assignments in their own courses, but it is likely to enhance peers' understanding of their purpose for the seminar. Once peer educators have this understanding, they are better able to help new students see the connection to course purpose and help dispel the idea that the assignments are merely busy work. Eventually, it may also cause them to re-evaluate their attitudes toward assignments in their own courses.

Instructors' Expectations of Student Behavior

Before assuming this role, peer educators may have sometimes exhibited behaviors inappropriate for the learning environment and for developing good working relationships with instructors, such as texting, accessing online social networks, reading the campus newspaper, talking to friends, sleeping, and otherwise failing to participate in class. They likely did not think twice about the negative effect of those behaviors on the learning environment or faculty perceptions of them. Yet, significant development for peer educators can occur as they begin to internalize instructors' expectations of students. Training, course planning, and facilitating the seminar provide opportunities for peer educators to gain greater insight into those expectations.

At some point during training, it is likely that one or more peer educators will exhibit some of the previously mentioned inappropriate behaviors. Program administrators' can use this as a teachable moment, engaging peer educators in a conversation about how they would feel if the first-year students in the courses they were teaching behaved in such a way. Such a conversation is the first step in getting peer educators to reconsider their own actions in the classroom. The second opportunity presents itself when peer educators and their co-instructors begin drafting course policies (i.e., class participation, attendance, communication with the instructors, respect for peers and instructors, expectations for classroom behavior). Here, peer educators may reflect on and begin to adjust their behavior in their own classes. Finally, as peer educators enter the classroom, they will no doubt observe and be expected to respond to inappropriate student behavior. Viewing these issues from the perspective of instructor rather than student can be a powerful learning experience.

Educational Outcomes Associated With Peer Education

Peer educators bring a range of prior experience to the role, but all have achieved some level of academic and social success that qualifies them for the position. Yet, many students choose to take on the peer leadership role to further enhance some of the same skills that qualified them for the position. They recognize the peer educator experience is an opportunity to practice and develop these skills, many of which are transferrable to other student leadership positions or future professional roles.

A 2009 study from the National Resource Center for The First-Year Experience and Students in Transition attempted to learn more about the peer leader experience and the outcomes associated with it. An invitation to participate in the Peer Leadership Survey was sent to 3,733 institutional representatives who were asked to forward the invitation to students serving as a peer leader. A total of 1,972 students at 414 institutions responded to the survey. While students served in peer leadership roles sponsored by a variety of campus units (e.g., orientation, residence life, community service offices, student government, athletics, religious organizations, counseling or mental health, judicial board), more than half of them (58.6%) served as peer educators in an academic unit. Respondents holding academic positions held a range of roles, including first-year seminar peer leader, tutor, academic mentor, peer advisor, and teaching assistant (Keup & Skipper, 2010). Here, we examine the responses of students serving in academic peer leader roles relative to the outcomes they attributed to their service.

Transferrable Skills

As a group, academic peer educators responding to the Peer Leadership Survey (National Resource Center, 2009) noted enhanced skills in a number of areas, many of which overlap with characteristics employers desire in new graduates (Table 2.1). As one survey respondent noted, "Being a peer leader has forced me to improve my time management and organizational skills. As a result ... I am much more organized in completing homework assignments and studying for exams" (National Resource Center, 2009). While organization and time management skills are essential for success in the workplace, many peers also saw immediate transfer to their academic experience. The next section will examine outcomes related to academic performance in greater depth.

Table 2.1

Skill Changes Associated With Academic Peer Leadership Experience (N = 998)

	Stronger or Much Stronger	
	Frequency	Percent
Interpersonal communication skills	948	95.0
Organization skills	799	80.1
Time management	790	79.2
Presentation skills	808	80.1

Academic Skills

In addition to personal management and communication skills, the Peer Leadership Survey revealed a positive relationship between the peer education experience and enhanced academic performance (National Resource Center, 2009). Nearly 60% of academic peer educators reported their academic performance was affected positively or very positively as a result of the peer leader experience. In particular, they noted improvements in written communication skills (62.5%) and general academic skills (56.1%). Responses to open-ended survey questions suggest that many peer educators spend extra time on their own skills in order to be better role models for the students they serve, as the following comments illustrate:

> I feel as though it has helped me stay on task as a student. Assisting others with time management skills is a great way to make sure I am following my own advice.

> It has caused me to continue to be a good role model for my students and "practice what I preach."

> While I was taking harder classes as a sophomore, I feel that I better managed them once I had gone through the peer leader training process. By setting an example for the incoming freshmen that I worked with, I helped myself achieve academic goals and become better at handling the stress of the work. (National Resource Center, 2009)

However, enhanced academic performance can also be attributed to peer educators' own learning within the first-year seminar. For example, engaging in class discussion and facilitating lessons related to a wide range of academic strategies may prompt peer educators to adopt these in their own lives. If peer educators teach new students about the impact of good time management on academic success and share suggested strategies (e.g., maintaining a calendar, planning in advance for projects and exams), they may be reminded of the effectiveness of those strategies and begin using them (or use them more consistently). If peer educators facilitate a lesson on improving study strategies, they will likely reflect on their own study strategies and may make adjustments in order to be able to share examples that have proven to be successful for them personally. Peers in a discipline-specific first-year seminar may find helping new students master the content reinforces and enhances their understanding of concepts learned previously. As one academic peer leader noted,

Leading my peers through material for their biology course allows me to review concepts that reappear in upper-level biology classes. I'm able to spend less time reviewing for my own courses because the material is still fresh in my head from discussions we have in the study group I lead. (National Resource Center, 2009)

Interpersonal Skills

The peer educator experience provides students with the opportunity to enhance relationships with a variety of campus constituents, in addition to increasing interactions with and understanding of people from diverse backgrounds. Responses of academic peer leaders reflected these enhanced relationships and better understanding of others (Table 2.2). When paired with improved communication skills, the peer leader experience may yield significant gains in interpersonal skills for those serving in this role.

Table 2.2
Peer Leader Outcomes Related to Interpersonal Skills (N = 998)

	Increased	
	Frequency	Percent
Meaningful interactions with peers	891	89.3
Meaningful interactions with faculty	853	85.5
Meaningful interactions with staff	849	85.1
Interactions with people of diverse backgrounds	777	77.6
Understanding people of diverse backgrounds	771	77.3

The Overall Collegiate Experience

In terms of peer educator success, the most important outcomes related to this experience may be increases in satisfaction and persistence (Table 2.3). The development of personal and academic skills results in peer educators being more successful overall in their other collegiate experiences, both inside and outside the classroom. For example, one student reflected on the role stating, "It has changed my entire schooling experience. I have no idea where I would be today without having been involved. I am better in every aspect of communication, vision, goal setting, etc." (National Resource Center, 2009). Additionally, in the process of informing first-year students about campus resources, peer educators often learn more about them and begin using the services for their own benefit. As one academic peer educator noted, "While teaching first-year students how to understand and take advantage of campus resources, I felt that I pushed myself to become more involved with them as well" (National Resource Center, 2009). Enhanced relationships with peers, faculty, and staff may lead to a greater sense of community and belonging for peer educators. One survey respondent stated, "I feel more connected to the community and more invested at the university"(National Resource Center, 2009). Feelings of belonging or connectedness to an institution have been found to be a significant factor in determining the retention and satisfaction of all students (Baker & Pomerantz, 2000; Latino, 2007).

Table 2.3
Peer Leadership Impact on the Overall Collegiate Experience (N = 998)

	Increased	
	Frequency	Percent
Knowledge of campus resources	899	90.1
Feeling of belonging at institution	790	79.2
Desire to persist at institution	697	69.8

Supporting Peer Educator Development

As the research presented in the previous section suggests, students see the peer educator experience contributing to their growth and development in a number of areas. Here, we offer suggestions for specific strategies for supporting student learning and development in the peer educator experience.

Assessing Peer Educators' Skills and Confidence Levels

To effectively attend to the development of peer educators throughout their experience, program administrators must first gain an understanding of peer educators' skills. Addressing students' initial competencies will inform training content, offering administrators insight into which baseline skills can be built on and highlighting critical skills that need development. Initial competencies can be assessed through the application and interview processes, particularly if an interactive, activity-based interview format is used (see chapter 3), and monitored throughout the experience by having the students reflect on their individual skill attainment. The Mentoring Confidence Inventory (Sanft et al., 2008) is one resource for guiding peer educator reflection. Using this inventory during training in preparation for the peer educator experience allows students to assess their confidence in the following areas:

» Becoming a peer mentor (i.e., defining and understanding mentorship)
» Helping students make the transition to college
» Defining roles (i.e., understanding the peer educator role)
» Establishing and maintaining relationships
» Understanding self-awareness
» Becoming a role model
» Developing cultural sensitivity
» Communicating effectively
» Facilitating learning
» Planning and problem solving
» Using campus resources
» Evaluating their own mentoring (i.e., ability to self-assess)

The inventory can be used as a pre-assessment tool to determine the current skill set of each individual peer educator and evaluate the cohort as a whole. It can also be part of a longitudinal assessment by comparing pre- and post-assessment results to gauge learning and development over the course of the term. (Additional evaluation and assessment strategies are presented in chapter 5.) Program administrators' understanding of the learning and development that takes place among peer educators throughout their experience will allow for better framing of the peer educator experience, enhanced training initiatives, and learning-centered assessment.

Training and Ongoing Support

Training initiatives, team building and course planning activities, and classroom facilitation all provide sites for the learning and development of students serving in a peer educator role. While training is addressed more extensively in chapter 4, we offer some specific strategies here to facilitate the development of the skills highlighted throughout this chapter.

Interpersonal skills. Devoting time in training to explaining effective interpersonal skills will allow peer educators to understand the importance of empathetic listening, use of nonverbal cues, and attentiveness for building trust between the peer and the first-year students served. These skills can be practiced in training through the use of role-play and/or small-group discussions that address case studies involving various interactions between peer educators and their students.

Training sessions might also discuss the multiple methods peer educators use to communicate with new students, including face-to-face conversation, text messages, phone calls, e-mails, and social media messages. As each of these media present challenges to effective communication, peer educators should be given practice in tailoring messages to fit the medium.

Presentation and facilitation skills. Much of the training will focus on explaining and role modeling appropriate pedagogy for the first-year seminar, with an emphasis on active learning and a demonstration of strategies that will assist in the achievement of learning goals. Examples of active-learning strategies are provided in chapter 4, and training can provide opportunities for role-playing these strategies and learning how to develop lesson plans that use such strategies.

In the classroom, peer educators refine their presentation skills as they deliver relevant content and facilitation skills by guiding students through icebreakers, activities, and discussions. Opportunities to debrief their teaching experiences with other peer leaders can further enhance skill development, as will constructive feedback from their co-instructor.

Goal setting, time management, and organizational skills. Goal setting is multifaceted for peer educators. They will set goals for their relationship with the co-instructors, their influence on the first-year students in their classes, and their personal achievements throughout the experience. The use of reflective writing in training will not only encourage peer educators to focus on setting goals and devising steps for accomplishing them but can enhance appropriate goal development.

Specifically, the work associated with coteaching the first-year seminar may include planning the syllabus, dividing up teaching tasks, managing attendance, developing effective lesson plans, and teaching and facilitating lessons. As such, the classroom experience offers ample opportunities for peer educators to engage in goal setting, effective organizational strategies, and time management.

Problem-solving and conflict-management skills. An important component of training will focus on navigating issues that peer educators will face in their experience coteaching the first-year seminar, including strategies for solving problems and managing conflict. While there is no way to predict every issue that peer educators will face throughout their experiences, feedback from peer educators who have previously served in the role at both the University of South Carolina and University of Kentucky suggests a common concern is balancing the roles of peer educator and friend in relation to the first-year students. Using case studies and veteran peer leader panels in training will introduce some of the problems peer educators might expect to encounter. Veteran peer leaders can suggest specific strategies for solving problems or managing conflicts, or peer educators can engage in role-plays or discussions to develop strategies.

Peer educators may meet with students one-on-one outside of class, assessing areas of concerns and recommending strategies for addressing those concerns. In many cases, this will involve connecting students to appropriate campus resources. All of these situations offer peer educators practice in problem solving and managing conflict, including enhancing their skills in determining what issues they are equipped to handle on their own versus those for which they will need assistance. Again, opportunities to debrief challenging situations with other peer leaders, program administrators, or the co-instructor are also valuable in helping peer educators assess and refine their performance.

Conclusion

The peer educator experience is a unique leadership opportunity allowing students to serve in various roles, and provide guidance to their peers through compassion and empathy, while acting with authority and promoting expectations consistent with college-level academic work. Additionally, this experience is heavily joined with a faculty or staff member. There are few opportunities for undergraduate students to work closely with a faculty member, as a colleague, for a full academic term.

It is important that program administrators and cooperative faculty and staff recognize the outcomes peer educators can experience from their service and create opportunities through training, practice, and reflection for peer educators to realize the full benefit of their service. The positive outcomes associated with peer education provide program administrators with a strong rationale for incorporating peers into the first-year seminar.

Chapter 3
Recruitment and Selection
of Peer Educators

Program administrators should consider that while the success of a peer educator program is dependent on many factors, finding student leaders who can fulfill the roles and responsibilities expected of peer educators in the classroom is critical. While peer educators can be trained in specific approaches to their expected roles and responsibilities, much care must be taken in recruiting and selecting students with the desire, commitment, and potential to meet program expectations. Therefore, adequate time and effort must be spent on creating detailed, effective, and efficient marketing, recruitment, and selection plans. Creation of these plans will include developing the profile of the ideal peer educator, determining compensation, crafting an application, formulating a comprehensive marketing plan that includes both passive and active recruitment strategies, setting selection criteria and policies, and deciding on an interview format.

Developing the Profile of the Ideal Peer Educator

The first step in recruiting and selecting peer educators is to determine the type of student leader desired. The profile of the ideal peer educator should guide decisions about the application and serve as the basis for marketing as well as the interview and selection processes. The exact profile will vary from institution to institution, and program to program, depending on the requirements of each individual seminar and institutional requirements for peer educators (e.g., minimum grade point average, hours earned). However, all program administrators can consider the following list of questions as a starting point for developing their peer educator profiles:

» Should peer educators be full-time students, only or are part-time students acceptable?

» Should the peer educator role be limited to undergraduate students, graduate students, or both?

» Additionally for undergraduates, should the role be restricted by classification (e.g., sophomores and upper-division students)?

» Should peer educators have previously taken the first-year seminar?

» What academic expectations should be set for peer educators? Should there be a grade point average (GPA) requirement?

» What campus involvement expectations (e.g., previous involvement, concurrent involvement, both) should be set for peer educators?

» What social and behavioral expectations should be set for peer educators? Which personalities seem best suited to those expectations?

» Is there a specific time commitment expected of peer educators (i.e., number of hours spent preparing for class; teaching in the classroom; attending meetings; and taking care of out-of-class duties, such as e-mail and grading)?

» What professional and personal characteristics should peer educators exhibit?

» What skills (e.g., ability to use discretion, maintain confidentiality, and display empathetic listening) should peer educators be able to exhibit prior to selection and training?

After considering these questions, program administrators can begin to craft the ideal peer educator profile, being sure to concentrate on program-specific requirements, such as the ability to attend training or teach at a particular time. Peer educator profiles can fall along a continuum, with very specific profiles lying at one end and more loosely defined profiles lying at the other. Many profiles will likely fall somewhere in between. There are advantages and disadvantages to both ends of the spectrum. More specific profiles better educate students on expectations for the role and are more likely to attract the type of student program administrators seek, yet they also leave little room for exceptions if followed strictly. On the other hand, more flexible profiles provide room for discretion in selecting students but cause confusion or lack of understanding pertaining to expectations. They can also attract students who do not match what program administrators truly desire. Following are examples of both types of profiles, which can be adapted to meet individual program needs.

More Specific Profile of a Peer Educator

Students applying to be a peer educator must

» Be a full-time, undergraduate student
» Possess and maintain a minimum 3.0 GPA
» Have and maintain a clear judicial record

To be selected for the peer educator role, students should demonstrate

» Depth and breadth of campus and community involvement, as well as the ability to articulate the importance of getting involved during the collegiate career
» Mature and informed decision making regarding social interactions, particularly involving alcohol
» A desire to mentor new students and ability to model effective academic and social success strategies
» Comfort in interacting with and relating to diverse student, faculty, and staff populations
» Enthusiasm for the university and the first-year seminar program, including the ability to articulate the benefits of the course
» Exemplary presentation, time management, and organizational skills
» Ability to commit adequate time and effort to fulfill the role (e.g., participation in required trainings, meetings, and preparation activities)

More Flexible Profile of a Peer Educator

Students applying for the peer educator role should be able to demonstrate

» Ability to succeed academically
» Involvement in campus activities and organizations
» Informed decision making and role modeling regarding social behavior
» Ability to connect with a diverse student population
» A desire to mentor new students

As the profiles are developed, administrators should consider how student leaders will demonstrate their ability to fit the profile through the application and/or interview processes. While suggestions on crafting the application and interview format follow, administrators will want to keep the profile statement in mind as they develop these processes.

Considering Compensation for Peer Educators

Prior to creating an application and marketing the position, program administrators should consider if, and how, they will compensate peer educators. In a recent survey of peer leaders (Keup & Skipper, 2010), 48.5% of respondents indicated they received some type of compensation for their peer educator role, with many receiving multiple forms of compensation (Table 3.1). The most common form of compensation is financial remuneration, though many receive course credit. Discussion on national listservs offered through the National Resource Center for The First-Year Experience and Students in Transition and the National Orientation Directors Association in January 2011 revealed a wide range of other forms of compensation, including a vast array of gifts and tokens of appreciation (i.e., clothing, portfolios, tote bags), end-of-semester banquets, awards, and letters of recommendation. Keup and Skipper (2010) noted that more than 50% of respondents indicated receiving no compensation (i.e., served voluntarily). Should program administrators choose to forgo compensation, they might consider what benefits they can promote to encourage intrinsic motivation and volunteer involvement, including, but not limited to, building leadership skills, developing relationships with faculty, enhancing résumés, and being able to give back to the university community. These benefits are further discussed in chapter 2.

Table 3.1

Compensation Received for Work as a Peer Leader ($N = 1,025$)

	Frequency	Percent
Financial compensation	705	68.8
No compensation	528	51.5
Course credit	311	30.3
Other compensation	54	5.3

Crafting the Peer Educator Application

No matter the institution or program, the primary component of any peer educator recruitment and selection process is typically an application. Applications serve multiple purposes, such as (a) offering an overview of the program; (b) informing potential peer educators of the roles and responsibilities associated with the position, as well as expectations for their involvement; (c) providing an avenue for collecting information about the applicants; and

(d) allowing applicants to demonstrate their eligibility for the position. Much like the variance in peer educator profiles, the format and components of applications will differ among institutions and programs dependent on specific requirements. Figures 3.1 and 3.2 offer a sample cover sheet and application from the first-year seminar peer leader program at the University of Kentucky. Specific and additional components are discussed in more detail below.

Cover Sheet

Applications should include a cover sheet (or have information posted on a web page) providing program details and adequately explaining to potential applicants the role for which they are applying. Common elements of the cover sheet include

» *Course overview.* For established programs, it is likely applicants will have previously taken the course and will therefore have an understanding of its purpose and organization. However, an overview is critical for programs that do not require peer educators to enroll in the course prior to serving in this leadership role.

» *Peer educator profile and/or program overview.* While the peer educator profile will explain the roles, responsibilities, expectations, and eligibility requirements for the position, the program description will provide a general understanding of position, its purpose, and where it falls in the institution's organizational chart. A program overview on a peer leader application might read

> Peer educators are integral to the success of U101: The First-Year Seminar. Peer educators are paired with faculty or staff course instructors to coteach the seminar. Peer educators support course instructors in teaching and facilitating lessons and interacting with students both inside and outside the classroom. Their primary responsibilities include serving as positive role models by providing the perspective of a successful student in relation to course topics and activities. Peer educators will be selected, trained, and supervised by the director of the Office of First-Year Student Services.

» *Explanation of compensation and/or benefits.* In addition to any monetary or in-kind compensation, it can be useful to advertise the benefits peer educators will gain from the experience to increase intrinsic motivation.

UK 101/UK 201 Peer Instructor Application
Return to 567 Patterson Office Tower by Friday, March 9, 2012 at 4:30 pm

---

Overview of UK 101:

UK 101 and UK 201 (www.uky.edu/UK101) are one-credit hour academic orientation courses for freshmen and transfer students cotaught by a faculty member and a student peer instructor. They are both offered during the first 10 weeks of the fall semester. Specific goals of UK 101 include helping students to understand the nature of a college education, acquire skills for achieving academic success, increase awareness and use of University resources, and experience small-group interaction with their peers, a faculty member, and a student peer instructor.

The Peer Instructor Position:

Peer Instructors are an essential component of UK 101 and UK 201. Responsibilities include assisting the faculty instructor, teaching class sessions, and interacting with the students during in-class and out-of-class activities. Much more information about the role of Peer Instructors can be found online at http://www.uky.edu/StudentAffairs/NewStudentPrograms/UK101/pdf/rolePeerInstructors.pdf.

Application Process:

If you are interested in applying for a UK 101 or UK 201 Peer Instructor position, please complete the following three-step application process. All applicants will be notified of their acceptance by April 20, 2012.

Step 1:   Complete and turn in the application to 567 Patterson Office Tower by Friday, March 9, 2012 at 4:30 pm. When you turn in your application, application, please sign up for an interview. (*Returning Peer Instructors are not required to interview, but must still complete Step 3 after registering for classes. Returners will be considered based on course and instructor evaluations from the previous year(s).*)

Step 2:   Interview for the position. Interviews will be held March 19, 20, 22, and 23 in the Student Center. Interviews are conducted in groups and last 1 hour and 15 minutes.

Step 3:   After you have registered for classes, complete and turn in the Availability Sheet to 567 Patterson Office Tower by no later than Friday, April 13, 2012 at 4:30 pm.

Figure 3.1. University of Kentucky peer instructor cover sheet. Used with permission.

Selection Process:

The following criteria are considered in the Peer Instructor selection process:

» We look for students with a proven academic track record. A cumulative GPA of a 3.0 or higher is preferred.

» We look for students who are involved on campus in multiple student organizations and can share with new students the process of getting involved on campus.

» We look for students who are good role models from a social standpoint. We look for students who make wise decisions in regards to alcohol consumption.

» We look for friendly students who can to connect with a variety of different types of students.

» We look for students who are enthusiastic about UK and the UK 101/201 experience.

» How well you do in your interview.

» Your availability to teach courses.

Training Requirements:

All Peer Instructors are required to attend two trainings.

1. **UK 101 Planning Workshop** (Must coordinate which session you'll be attending with your co-instructor.)

   All planning workshops will be held in 230 Student Center. Mon, April 23 from 12 – 3 pm; Wed, April 25 from 9 am – 12 pm; Thurs, April 26 from 2 – 5 pm

2. **UK 101 Peer Instructor Fall Training**

   Saturday, August 25 from 10 am – 4 pm in 230 Student Center. Lunch will be provided.

   If you have any questions, please call 859-257-6597.

Figure 3.1 continues.

UK 101/UK 201 Peer Instructor Application

Return applications to 567 Patterson Office Tower by 4:30 pm on Friday, March 9, 2012. Sign up for an interview if you are a new applicant. Group interviews will be held March 19, 20, 22, and 23 and last 1 hour and 15 minutes.

Name:_____ Student ID#:_____

LinkBlue User ID:_____ Sex: Male Female

Phone #:_____ Email Address:_____

Major:_____ Minor:_____ Cumulative GPA:_____

Classificatoin in Fall 2011: SO JR SR T-shirt Size: S M L XL XXL

Are you a first-generation student? Yes No Were you a transfer student? Yes No

Returning Peer Instructor Applicants

Returning peer instructor applicants are NOT required to submit answers to the essay questions nor are they required to interview again. Simply return your application 567 Patterson Office Tower by Friday, March 9, 2012 at 4:30 pm and then turn in your Availability Sheet to 567 POT by Friday, April 13, 2012.

New Peer Instructor Applicants

Please indicate which class you'd prefer to teach: UK 101 _____ UK 201 _____

Either _____

Did you take UK 101? Yes_____ No_____ Did you take UK 201? Yes_____ No_____

Students Oraganizations/Campus Activities:_____

_____

Campus References (e.g., professor, Hall Director, adminstrator) Please list at least one.

	Name	Position	Phone Number
1.			
2.			

Essay Questions (Please type your answers and attach them as a seperate page)

1. What is one piece of advice you wish you had been given your first semester of college.
2. Describe three positive attributes about yourself and explain how they will contribute to your effective.

Please Read and Sign the Following:

By signing this application, I certify that the above information is true and accurate to the best of my knowledge. I also understand that my signature gives the Office of New Student & Parent Programs permission to verify my grade point average. I have read and understood the expectations outlined in the UK 101/201 Peer Instructor application. I also verify by signing that I can attend all training sessions and meetings outlined in the application. I verify that I have a clear discipline record and am in good standing with the University of Kentucky.

Signature _____ Date _____

FOR OFFICE USE: Date In _____ Grades Checked _____ *UK 101 PI Application 2012: NSPP Leadership Site*

Figure 3.2. University of Kentucky peer instructor application. Used with permission.

» *Training and program requirements.* Clearly listing this information on the cover sheet and indicating where attendance is mandatory may eliminate the possibility of selecting candidates with schedule conflicts. It is recommended that applicants put these mandatory requirements in their planners in anticipation of selection.

» *Application and selection process and timeline.* Listing this information in advance can avoid repetitive phone calls and e-mails to the program office. Suggestions for developing and implementing a selection process can be found later in this chapter.

Application Form

In addition to a request for demographic information, an application form may also incorporate the following components depending on the selection process:

» *Essay questions.* Answers to essay questions can provide vital information about applicants and their qualifications. Further, essay questions can provide background information that can supplement or expand on information during the interview process. Sample essay questions include

• Why do you want to be a peer educator?

• Looking back on your first year of college, what would you now consider to be two strategies for making a successful transition that you wish you would have known?

• Describe how you are involved on campus and how that may impact your effectiveness in coteaching the first-year seminar.

• What would you consider to be the two most common transition issues new students face, and how would you address those in the first-year seminar?

• Describe three positive attributes you possess and how those attributes would enhance your role as a peer educator.

» *Request for references.* If references are asked for, it is recommended they come from campus professionals (e.g., staff supervisors, advisors, faculty who have taught them) who can speak to the student's academic success and/or campus involvement, both of which are relevant to the position. References can be useful to differentiate between applicants in the final stages of the selection process.

» *Verification statement.* It is helpful to include a statement that asks students to verify the information they have provided is true and accurate and that they understand the roles, responsibilities, and commitments of a peer educator. In addition, permission can be obtained to verify grades and audit disciplinary records.

Depending on the selection process and the first-year seminar offerings, the application form may also ask for interview time preferences (or unavailability, if choices are offered) and course section preferences and/or eligibility to teach special sections (e.g., business majors serving as peer educators in seminars with a business focus or theme). To assist with pairing peer educators with sections and instructors, it can be useful to list the days of the week and times the seminar is offered and ask applicants to mark their availability if this information is known in advance.

Marketing Strategies for Recruiting Peer Educators

After the application is crafted, it is time to start thinking about how to get it in the hands of as many eligible students as possible. For numerous reasons, including limited time and budgets, marketing often does not receive the attention it deserves. However, it should be remembered that the long-term success of the program depends on a sustained number of quality applicants. Much effort should be put into the best avenues for reaching a diverse and wide range of students, especially for those programs that often see the same small population of students serving in all of the leadership positions on campus. While peer educator programs assist first-year students, they also develop leaders on campus; therefore, marketing must be far-reaching and attractive.

One challenge with marketing on a college campus is that today's students are overwhelmed by and inundated with information. Thus, it becomes important to make the message the program is sending stand out. While there are many ways to do this, the key to success is to remember that students' perception of importance will be affected by how much attention a message is given. If they receive one message about applying to be a peer educator, it likely will not seem important. However, if they receive many messages from multiple sources over a period of time, the perceived importance increases. Some students might be annoyed in the short term by the barrage of advertisement, but others might rethink their original dismissal of the opportunity, as evidenced by this University of Kentucky student's comment, "Well I wasn't going to apply but after getting the eighth e-mail and third flier about it, I figured I should give it a shot."

Avenues for Marketing the Peer Educator Application

The avenues for marketing on each campus will vary depending on policies, programs, and partnerships. The options described below can jump start the formulation of any marketing plan.

E-mail campaign. E-mail is the easiest and most cost-efficient way to communicate with students and campus partners. It is simple, fast, and can be used to reach a wide range of people. However, today's students, faculty, and staff are overwhelmed by e-mail, and every new message that comes in is probably less likely to be read than the one before. Therefore, the following tips should be kept in mind for an effective e-mail campaign:

» Keep e-mails brief. Provide web links to additional information if necessary.
» Personalize e-mails when possible.
» Keep e-mails simple and in a format that can be easily read and viewed on a variety of electronic devices.
» Attach the application in a portable document format (PDF) to prevent the application from being altered and to ensure document capability across a range of computing platforms.
» Remember, one e-mail will not suffice in getting the message out. Plan a schedule of reminder messages throughout the recruitment period.

Campus media campaign. There are many opportunities to include information about the peer educator position and application process in print and electronic media outlets on campus. These include

» **Table tents.** If a unit on your campus coordinates fliers that are put on tables in campus dining facilities, libraries, and other campus hot spots, program coordinators can ask to include an ad announcing the recruitment dates. If no one coordinates this for the campus, the seminar organizers can seek permission to create and distribute their own announcement.
» **Stall Stories or Potty Talk.** Many campuses take advantage of the inside of bathroom stalls in residence halls and popular classroom buildings to

post important notices for students. As with table tents, these may be coordinated by a central office. If so, program administrators can place an ad in the newsletter.

» **Posters** advertising recruitment can be hung in residence hall lobbies and individual floors as well as on bulletin boards throughout campus.

» **Newspaper ad or story.** The program administrator should contact the campus newspaper to see if the editor will consider running a story on the program just before or during the recruitment period (preferably on the front page). To make the story more interesting for students, current peer educators could be interviewed. The program coordinator can also consider purchasing an ad to promote the program.

» **Campus media.** Campus radio and television stations frequently run public service announcements (PSA) for events with broad appeal to the institutional community. The program coordinator should check to see if a PSA is a possibility. In some cases, station managers might also arrange for the seminar director or selected peer leaders to be interviewed on air.

» **Institutional homepage.** While recruitment information should have a prominent location on the seminar and/or peer educator program website, the program coordinator might also look into the possibility of having a banner ad, announcement, feature article, or video posted to the college or university's homepage. The office of public relations for the institution is a logical place to start in trying to get real estate on the main page.

Social media campaign. Today's students spend a large amount of time on social networks to maintain friendships, communicate with peers, organize and plan events, and find out campus and world news. Given these uses, social networks may be one of the best avenues for recruiting students. Below are strategies for three of the most popular social networks—Facebook, Twitter, and YouTube.

» Facebook provides multiple opportunities for promoting the first-year seminar and peer educator program.

• Create a fan page for the first-year seminar and/or peer educator program, and use it to post announcements and advertise the peer educator position. Current peer educators, instructors, and campus partners who are on Facebook can be asked to encourage others to *like* the page, enabling them to see announcements and advertisements.

- Create an event through the fan page that tells students how to obtain an application and the deadline to apply. Encourage Facebook fans, current peer educators and instructors, and campus partners to invite others to attend the event.

- Create an ad through the fan page that can be targeted to students in the institutional network based on various demographics. The ad will show up in the sidebar of those individual students' Facebook accounts and can be linked to additional information.

- Encourage current peer educators, instructors, and campus partners to share information about the peer educator program and its Facebook fan page on their individual, departmental, and/or program pages through wall posts, status updates, and notes, all including links to the application.

» Twitter can also be used as a promotional tool for the first-year seminar and/or peer educator program. Post tweets that include links to the application and encourage current peer educators, instructors, and campus partners with Twitter accounts to retweet the posts.

» YouTube has created many Internet sensations, and often the silliest, lowest-quality videos turn into the greatest hits. Videos promoting the program can be posted to the site and then shared on other social networks, in e-mails, and on websites.

Other marketing opportunities. In addition to the aforementioned promotional strategies, the following options may also be considered:

» Solicit recommendations from faculty, staff, and other student leaders, particularly those connected with the first-year seminar.

» Work with campus partners to post links to the application and information about the program to various campus websites.

» Attend student organization meetings to promote the position and distribute applications.

» Staff information tables at popular locations on campus (e.g., dining facilities, residence halls, major classroom buildings, main walkways) and hand out fliers and copies of the application. Consider including a Quick Response (QR) code, a custom two-dimensional matrix barcode, on the flier that links directly to an online version of the application.

» Chalk blackboards in popular classroom buildings and ask professors of courses with large enrollments for time to make announcements to students before class.
» Hold informational sessions for students to learn more about the position and obtain a copy of the application.
» Put copies of applications at the front desks of popular campus offices.

Strategies for Interviewing Peer Educator Candidates

While some program administrators will use only the application to select peer educators, others will interview the applicants in some fashion to supplement the application. Interviews provide an opportunity to see how candidates interact in person, rather than just how they respond on paper. How interviews are structured will depend on a variety of factors, including the size of the applicant pool, the amount of time available to interview candidates, the staff support available to interview candidates, the purpose of the interviews, and the personal preferences of the program administrators. Interviews can be done one-on-one or in groups, be question- or activity-based, and can last a few minutes to several hours.

Deciding on an Interview Format

When deciding on an interview format, program administrators will want to take many of the aforementioned variables into consideration. The following questions will help guide the formulation of an interview format, plan, and schedule:

» Number of applicants
  • What is the size of the applicant pool?
  • Is it realistic, in terms of time and resources, to interview each applicant individually, or should interviews be conducted in groups?
» Purpose of interview
  • Is the purpose to get additional details about information presented on the application? If so, individual interviews may be the best option.
  • Is the purpose to get a sense of how candidates will interact with others? If so, then perhaps a group interview of some type is best.
  • Is the purpose to gain insight into what candidates think? If so, a traditional question-based interview format may work best.

- Is the purpose to have candidates demonstrate specific skills? If so, an activity-based or interactive interview may be the best choice.

» Format of interview
  - Who will be involved in selecting the cohort?
    - Will the program administrators conduct all interviews, or will others help?
    - How will this affect the format of the interview?
    - If multiple interviewers are involved, how will consistency across interviews be ensured?
  - What space is available to conduct the interviews?
    - Does this determine interview timing?
    - Does this impact interview format?

Question-Based Interviews

If a question-based format is used, questions should be derived from the roles, responsibilities, and expectations of the peer educator position. The goal is for candidates to demonstrate an understanding of the position and the purpose it serves, as well as to demonstrate how they fit the role. Questions should be open-ended and vary in type. Suggested interview questions include

» How do you plan to impact the first-year students and aid in their transition to campus?

» What concerns do you have about fulfilling the peer educator role, and how do you plan to overcome those concerns?

» Reflecting on your experience as a first-year student, what is the most important lesson you learned that you would share with the new students in your class?

» Imagine you are out at party and see one of the students from your class. She is drinking, and you know she is underage. What do you do?

» Describe a past experience working with a partner. How would that experience translate to working with your co-instructor in team teaching the first-year seminar?

There are advantages and disadvantages to each type of interview format. The traditional, question-based format can be used for one-on-one or group interviews, can be easily adapted for time constraints, can be conducted in a variety of locations, ensures consistency across interviews, and gives the interviewer a sense of applicants' communication and critical-thinking skills. However, this format also presents some challenges in that it limits responses to an articulation rather than a demonstration of skills, and it can often lead to repetitive answers from applicants in group interview settings.

Interactive, Activity-Based Format

If time, space, and staffing permit, activity-based interviews offer program administrators a chance to observe candidates interact and showcase skills and talents. Examples of interactive activities that can assess the candidates' institutional and peer educator program knowledge; ability to think on their feet; presentation, facilitation, and conflict management skills; and diversity understanding include

» *Random draw.* Candidates draw a random university or program-related topic out of a bowl and must immediately present a one-minute lesson on the topic.

» *Pick the cohort.* A group of candidates are given profiles of 20 potential peer educators. Collectively they must agree upon the five candidates they would hire and their rationale for choosing these five candidates.

» *Sell the first-year seminar.* A group of candidates are instructed to create a two-minute commercial that sells the first-year seminar to new students. They are given a box of props, told that each candidate must have a speaking role, and that they must incorporate a specific list of random words into the commercial.

» *Sticky situations.* Candidates are presented with a sticky situation (e.g., a student not turning in assignments, engaging in underage drinking, or being disruptive in class). They are given a few moments to assess the situation and present a plan for addressing the situation.

» *Difficult questions.* Candidates are asked difficult questions from interviewers pretending to be new students in the first-year seminar (e.g., I know you are underage, but do you drink? How much time do you actually spend studying? Can I ask you out?), and they must give their best answers.

Selecting the Peer Educator Cohort

Once applications have been turned in and interviews (if applicable) are complete, it is time to select the cohort. Ideally, there will be more applications received than are needed to staff sections to allow for the selection of the best-qualified candidates. However, if too few applications are received, the program administrator will need to consider several critical questions, such as (a) are there applicants who could handle coteaching more than one section; (b) is it better to have a less-qualified peer educator in the classroom than no peer; (c) should sections be cut or combined to accommodate the available number of peer educators; and/or (d) if sections are not cut, which instructors will be assigned a peer and what criteria will be used in making that decision? While the hope is that these questions will not need to be addressed, it may be beneficial to consider them in advance and develop contingency plans to try to meet program goals while ensuring that each student who is selected can fulfill the role.

Conclusion

A peer educator program cannot be successful if it cannot sustain a cohort of highly qualified student leaders. Therefore, much time and effort must go into planning for recruitment and selection. The most important step in this process is developing the peer educator profile, as it determines the type of student one is looking for and informs all other steps of the recruitment and selection process. Prior to promoting the position, great care should be given to formulating a compensation plan (if desired), crafting an application, and developing a marketing plan. Once applications are collected, a variety of interviewing strategies can be used to learn more about the applicants before selecting the cohort. Selection should be tied to the peer educator profile, ensuring that the cohort selected is well suited to achieve program goals.

Chapter 4
Peer Educator Training and Development

The most time- and resource-consuming component of a peer leadership program is the training and development process. According to Newton and Ender (2010), the position of peer educator includes an intentional training effort to prepare the peers for their role. Training programs deliberately designed to provide information and practice essential to the job functions of peer educators will result in more effective peer leadership and enhance the efficacy of the first-year seminar. Program administrators should devote as much time to the training of peer leaders as they do to training and development of instructors.

In the Peer Leadership Survey (National Resource Center, 2009), 83.6% of respondents had participated in training to prepare them for their leadership roles. The length of training programs varied greatly across roles for academic peer leaders and campuses, ranging from a half-day or less (16.9%) to as much as one week (25.0%, Table 4.1). These data suggest that many programs rely on one-shot training efforts to prepare students for the peer leadership role. Yet, this approach can present challenges, as the diverse responsibilities of the peer leader position may be hard to cover thoroughly in a brief training event. It is also difficult to anticipate the challenges that peers may face given the unpredictability of first-year students and their transitions. Rosenthal and Shinebarger (2010) recommend "training and regular supervision continue throughout the year in the form of weekly group meetings to discuss workshops and students, and to brainstorm and plan" (p. 25). Placing significant emphasis on the development of peer leaders illustrates the value they bring to the first-year seminar classroom and signals a commitment to the development process of the peers serving in this role.

Table 4.1
Length of Training for Peer Leader Position ($N = 881$)

	Frequency	Percent
Half day or less	149	16.9
1 day	147	16.7
2 days	163	18.5
3 days	96	10.9
4 days	64	7.3
1 week	220	25.0
Other	310	35.2

Developing a Peer Leader Training Program

Peer leader training programs often serve two purposes: (a) to prepare students for their role in the classroom and (b) to provide an opportunity for them to participate in a leadership learning experience. Training programs should be developed based on the goals and learning outcomes of the first-year seminar as well as the goals and outcomes for the peer leadership program. As such, training programs should focus not only on the needs of first-year students but also on the potential leadership development of the peer educator.

Learning Objectives

One of the first steps in developing an effective peer leader training program is to identify the desired outcomes for the session. At a minimum, the content and processes for the training should be developed based on the answers to the question, What do I want the participants to know or be able to do as a result of this workshop? Identifying and communicating learning outcomes for training activities benefits the participants because they will have a clear idea of the purpose and goals for the session. Learning outcomes also benefit the program, as they provide a basis for assessment of the training.

It can be difficult to determine the cause-and-effect relationship between the training experience and outcomes that are not specific or encompass multiple areas of measurement. Thus, learning outcomes should be measurable. An example of a poorly developed statement of a learning outcome is,

As a result of this training, peer leaders will develop critical thinking skills.

Critical thinking skills, aside from being both broad and vague, are difficult to attribute to just one experience. A more measurable look at critical thinking may be,

As a result of this training, peer leaders will apply the principles of Bloom's Taxonomy of Critical Thinking in classroom situations.

This outcome is observable and measureable. A co-instructor or program administrator can observe a peer educator using his or her critical-thinking skills. This can be done at various points throughout the semester to better gauge the impact that training has had on the peers' use of these particular skills and application of Bloom's model. The development and assessment of learning outcomes will be further explored in chapter 5.

In addition to being measurable, learning outcomes should be written in a clear and concise manner. Awkwardly worded or poorly conceptualized outcomes are difficult to measure and fail to provide participants with a clear idea of what the training is designed to achieve, as the following statement illustrates:

As a result of participating in self-reflective exercises and discussions, peer leaders will be able to identify and apply helping strategies appropriate to different situations.

The following example presents a more manageable outcome providing clarity for the learner as well as effective measurement for the program administrators:

As a result of participating in self-reflective exercises, peer leaders will be able to describe helping strategies appropriate to the experience of first-year students.

If the training program has multiple components (i.e., multiday event, training course, workshop series), learning outcomes should be developed and articulated for each component. In addition to stating the outcomes, administrators should provide clarity for how these outcomes fit into the overall goals for the program.

A Framework for Developing a Training Program

One approach to developing a peer leader training program is to mirror the first-year seminar classroom experience. Gardner (1981) provided a framework for developing a first-year seminar classroom experience that can easily be adapted for a peer leader development program. His four-phase model outlines the processes through which a learning environment develops (Figure 4.1).

Four Phases

1. *Group Building / Developing Community*
   - » Increases group cohesiveness
   - » Increases level of trust within group
   - » Reduces anxiety levels in individuals
   - » Eliminates communication barriers

2. *Identifying Learner Needs and Characteristics*
   - » Focuses on goals
   - » Individualizes training
   - » Increases buy-in of group members

3. *Resource Discovery and Use*
   - » Recognizes resources within the group
   - » Identifies campus and community resources
   - » Provides ideas for learning applications
   - » Empowers participants

4. *Bridging and Transition*
   - » Creates structure for reflection and evaluation
   - » Moves learning from abstract to application
   - » Provides opportunity for goal setting
   - » Enables learning to extend beyond workshop

Figure 4.1. Four phases: An adaptable model for first-year seminar faculty development. Adapted from "Developing Faculty as Facilitators and Mentors" by J. N. Gardner, 1981, in V. A. Harren, M. H. Daniels, & J. N. Buch (Eds.), Facilitating students' career development (New Directions for Student Services No. 14, p. 67-80). Copyright 1981 by Wiley Periodicals.

Phase 1: Group Building / Developing Community. In the first phase, there is a focus on developing the community. Just as in a first-year seminar classroom, a training program—no matter the length—should provide opportunities for participants to get to know one another and build trust with the group. During this phase, the facilitator builds the foundation for the group. The first phase should not be abandoned after the start of the experience but rather continued throughout the training, intentionally moving through more intense experiences and pushing the group toward a stronger community as the experience progresses.

Facilitators can best develop the participants in this phase through experiential activities. Using community-building techniques that are applicable to the first-year seminar classroom allows the participants to make connections with their fellow participants while also learning strategies they can then apply in their roles as facilitators of the first-year seminar classroom.

Phase 2: Identifying Learner Needs and Characteristics. The second phase encourages the facilitator to determine the specific needs of the participants. While there is a common purpose for the group—to prepare for the peer leader role—participants arrive with a variety of needs, abilities, and motivations. Exploring their individual goals and identifying how their needs will be met through the role of peer leadership will increase the buy-in of the participants. Participants who recognize personal benefits from a training experience are more likely to be actively involved and to look favorably upon the experience.

Methods for determining the needs of training participants include goals assessments and sharing of expectations. Students show interest in the role of peer educator for a variety of reasons. Having participants articulate what they hope to gain from their experience as peer leaders can help facilitators align the program with participant expectations. Once the expectations are reviewed, facilitators can share with the participants the alignment with their personal goals and the outcomes of the peer leadership experience. Collecting this type of information from the peers as part of the training process also allows the training facilitators an opportunity to identify content they may have overlooked or a component of training that needs to be added or adapted to better align with the needs of the participants.

Phase 3: Resource Discovery and Use. In this phase, training participants are able to fill their toolbox with information and ideas that can be used in their role. These ideas should come from participants and facilitators, as participants who are invited to share their ideas will be more engaged in the training process and feel more prepared and empowered for their role as a peer leader.

This phase of training should closely reflect the program outcomes and should continue the experiential exploration of ideas and applications for the first-year seminar classroom. For example, providing an orientation to campus resources and services was identified as one of the three most important course objectives for the first-year seminar by more than 45% of the respondents to the 2009 National Survey of First-Year Seminars (Padgett & Keup, 2011). Alignment between seminar goals and peer leader training would suggest a focus on campus and community resources available for first-year students. In addition to knowing about campus resources, peer leaders should also receive training on appropriate referral strategies.

Phase 4: Bridging and Transition. Training programs packed with information and ideas can be overwhelming for participants. Providing an opportunity to reflect on the information presented and consider how it can be translated into the first-year seminar classroom can help the peer transition from a learner to a facilitator. Reflective practice in the training also helps build participants' confidence in their ability to succeed as peer leaders.

Often, we place reflection and evaluation at the end of a workshop. For workshops focused on just one topic, this may be effective. However, most training sessions are filled with information on a variety of topics. Creating a structure where participants are able to reflect on content throughout the workshop rather than only at the end will allow for greater clarity and understanding. As such, program administrators should consider including time and space for reflection and discussion about the application of each content area on the training agenda. This will allow participants to continually see the value of the information presented and build their understanding of how to apply what they have learned to their roles as peer leaders.

Content and Facilitation

After developing learning outcomes for the training experience, development of content and facilitation processes should follow. As with most training components, the content of a training program will vary based on the goals of the programs and the expectations of the peer leaders. The topics discussed here encompass a broad range of program types. Program administrators should consider how these general topics fit into their training program and what concepts specific to their program should supplement these more general ones.

Expectations. The roles and responsibilities of peer leaders may be presented through the recruitment and selection process. However, once the cohort has been selected and assembled for training, it is important for the program administration to present the expectations of students serving in the peer leader role. Expectations can be articulated in a variety of ways, including the use of veteran peer leaders; discussion about mutual expectations between peer leaders, instructors, and program administrators; and a presentation of the history and goals of the program.

History and goals of the program. Providing a historical context of the peer leader program, why and when it was developed, and the success that the program has seen, can build loyalty and commitment among new peer leaders. Hunter and Heath (2001) argue, "new peer leaders should understand the program's impact on student retention, the philosophy and history of the program, as well as program goals" (p. 46). Providing this background information as well as the current goals for the program can inspire a new cohort of students to leave their own legacy through their service as a peer leader.

Needs and challenges of first-year learners. Peer leaders have a distinct understanding of the students they serve due to their own recent experiences as first-year students. Yet, they may need to be reminded that every student experiences the transition to college in a unique way, and the emotions and challenges they faced may not be the same for the students in their course. It is important, therefore, to provide an overview of student needs anchored in data and theory. Providing an overview of the demographics, interests, expectations, and abilities of the current first-year class can help peer leaders anticipate the needs new students may present. This type of overview can be developed using campus-specific data from instruments such as the Cooperative Institutional Research Program's (CIRP) Freshman Survey, the National Survey on Student Engagement (NSSE), as well as campus-specific admissions reports. In addition to institution-specific information, a plethora of literature exists on the development of first-year students. Providing a short reading on the developmental process of first-year students or a selection on student development theory can provide peer educators with a more general understanding of the needs of first-year students (see list of recommended readings at the end of this chapter).

Course content. If peer leaders are expected to help deliver the content of the first-year seminar, they must have a clear understanding of the goals and outcomes of the seminar. Many peer leaders have likely taken the first-year seminar and may think they understand the course goals. However, responsibility for facilitating learning around the first-year seminar outcomes requires a more thorough understanding of the course than is likely achieved as a student in the course. Also, seminar outcomes may have changed since the peer was enrolled and any updates will need to be highlighted and shared.

One method for helping gauge students' understanding of course content is to have them develop a model lesson plan. Training facilitators can provide a basic template for a lesson plan and charge peer leaders with developing a lesson that addresses one or more course outcomes. This type of activity may also help build peer leaders' confidence in approaching their team instructor with ideas by giving them a framework through which they can identify and support their ideas.

Appropriate pedagogy. The training process is a perfect laboratory to demonstrate appropriate pedagogy for the first-year seminar classroom. Effective training sessions include a presentation of the importance of active learning as well as demonstrations of strategies that assist in the achievement of training goals and can be applied to the content of the first-year seminar. Some examples of active-learning strategies that can be used for training situations as well as in the classroom include

- » **Social barometer.** Participants or students are prompted to take a stand in the room based on their opinions about a particular topic.
- » **Think-pair-share.** Facilitators present questions to a large group by asking participants to first think about their own answer and make a few notes to capture their initial thoughts. Participants then pair up with a peer and discuss what they wrote during their individual think time. Pairs are then invited to share the key points of their conversation. This process allows all students to share their thoughts with someone and can be more comfortable for some students than volunteering to respond to a question presented to the full group.
- » **60-60-30-30.** Partners take turns talking for 60 seconds about a specific topic. A second round follows with a 30-second time limit for each partner.
- » **Film or television clips.** Using popular media is an effective way to prompt discussion about a topic or concept. For example, the facilitator may select movie clips to demonstrate movement through various phases of student development.
- » **Reflective writing.** Informal and/or ungraded writing assignments that provide an opportunity for students to reflect on information presented through a course or training experience can be as engaging as an activity where they are moving around the room. Quick one-minute papers or multiple writing prompts can help students apply what they have learned to their lives and unique personal experiences.

» **Games.** Measuring student learning through a game format can help liven up a training or classroom setting as well as provide evidence that learners understand presented content. Competition is also a great motivator for students.

» **Role-play.** Since training for peer leaders often takes place in the absence of first-year students, role-playing can be an effective method of practicing interactions with students. Role-play allows students to practice their skills and receive immediate feedback from peers and facilitators.

» **Peer panel.** Involving veteran peer leaders in the training of new leaders can be an effective way to build enthusiasm for the program as well as present expectations and responsibilities through honest perspectives. Seasoned peer leaders can be invited to share their experiences through a panel discussion. Panelists should be prompted with questions relevant to the training content being shared, and training participants should be invited and encouraged to ask questions of their peers. Hearing from peers in this way may ease concerns and increase confidence in new peers.

Challenging situations. Peer leadership is a multifaceted leadership opportunity. Peer leaders are expected to play the role of mentor, friend, liaison, confidant, teacher, and role model. Maintaining these various relationships can be challenging. Training programs should include time and methods to address the challenges that may accompany the peer leader role. The following suggested strategies can be adapted to a wide range of issues that may arise during the peer leader experience:

» **Negotiating the role of leader and friend.** One of the greatest challenges of the peer-to-peer learning process is establishing a relationship that places the peer educator in a role of authority, yet friend; instructor, yet confidant. Negotiating this role is one of the greatest challenges that peer leaders face. Many factors affect this relationship. For example, peer leaders and first-year students may be in the same clubs, organizations, or classes. A variety of strategies can be employed to address challenging situations (i.e., interaction with peers in a social setting, observation of first-year students engaged in risky behavior, attraction toward or from a first-year student). Role-playing can be an effective method to address these types of challenges. A panel of veteran peer leaders who faced and overcame difficult interactions with students can share their perspectives and facilitate a conversation based on their lessons learned.

» **Responding to the needs of first-year students.** Students in the peer leader role do not always anticipate the various needs first-year students have or the types of assistance they seek from the peer leader. Skills such as exercising compassion and empathy, reserving judgment, making appropriate referrals, and maintaining confidentiality are important but often difficult to observe in a training situation. To demonstrate these skills, training participants can be placed in groups and presented with a case study in which first-year students are facing difficulty. Groups work together to develop a strategy for assisting the student and share their strategy with the larger training group.

» **Building relationships between peer leaders and instructors.** One of the most unique components of the peer leadership role is the opportunity to work closely with a faculty or staff member serving as the course instructor. This relationship is likely different from any relationship a peer has had with an instructor, and peers may need some support in navigating their place in the teaching partnership. Training activities that approach building and sustaining an effective teaching partnership should be shared early on and throughout the experience since peers may face new challenges as they continue in their role. Veteran peer leaders and instructors can provide valuable insights into how to approach the relationship between instructor and peer leader. New programs may want to consider engaging campus partners who have established peer education programs and invite those teams to share their perspective. While the content of the first-year seminar is unique, the process of developing an effective partnership between faculty or staff and peer educator is shared across many programs. Other methods for helping peers build confidence in contributing to the teaching partnership include role-play, case study discussions, and interviews with experienced instructors.

Interpersonal communication. Students' success in the peer leadership role is dependent upon their ability to relate to their peers with a delicate balance of compassion and authority. Understanding and demonstrating appropriate use of key communication skills, such as empathetic listening, nonverbal cues, and attentiveness are essential for building trust between the peer and the learner.

Newton and Ender (2010; Ender & Newton, 2000) provide a framework for effective communication between peer leaders and students through the lens of helping skills. Many students are attracted to mentoring roles because they want to give advice to new students and help new students learn from their mistakes. Giving advice, however, is an ineffective way to assist new students in their development as independent learners. An introduction to helping skills specific to peer mentorship is an essential component of training to help peer leaders understand how they can benefit new students by helping them help themselves. According to Newton and Ender, helping skills allow the peer leader to "draw out the underlying concerns—which the student may well not have recognized—and provide support while the student works out ways to deal with them" (p. 99).

The concept of helping others help themselves may not come easily to peers, especially those who were drawn to the peer educator role by a desire to share their experiences and lessons learned with new students. For example, when giving advice, peers would talk *to* a student; whereas, in effective interpersonal communication—or using helping skills—the peer talks *with* the student. By comparing advice giving to effective interpersonal communication (Table 4.2), program administrators help peer educators learn the importance of letting new students make their own choices, and perhaps their own mistakes, rather than imposing their opinions upon students who are easily influenced.

Leadership learning. Service as a peer educator brings many benefits to the peer. Among these benefits is development of leadership skills. Leadership learning is best achieved when anchored in an experience or experiences where skills can be applied and practiced. The peer leadership role provides an ideal arena for students to learn about leadership development theories through the training process and then practice leadership in their role as a mentor, confidant, teacher, and authority figure in the first-year seminar classroom. With the support of a co-instructor and program administrators, students have an environment where they can safely practice leadership skills and develop their leadership style in a safe and supportive environment.

Presenting leadership theory as part of the training process, in a format that is relevant to the role of a first-year seminar peer leader, provides the learners

Table 4.2

Comparing Advice Giving to Interpersonal Communication

Variable	Advice giving	Interpersonal communication
Interaction	Directed (talking to)	Collaborative (talking with)
Helper's role	Authority	Facilitator
Expertise	Reliable knowledge	Interpersonal relation skills
Time	Brief and direct	Extended for exploration
Function	Provides necessary information	Assists individual problem solving
Relationship	Limited (courteous)	In-depth (interpersonal skills)
Precautions		
	Advice does not always fit the perspective or need of another	Requires having accurate listening and attending skills
Limits	Must have specific knowledge	Must understand when professional assistance is needed
Outcome	Not known	Outcome can be determined

Note. Reprinted from *Students Helping Students: A Guide for Peer Educators on College Campuses* (2nd ed.) by F. B. Newton & S. C. Ender, 2010, p. 98. Copyright 2010 by Jossey-Bass.

with a way to organize and make sense of their experiences. For example, Kouzes and Posner's (2002, 2007) Leadership Challenge is a leadership theory that can be easily related to the peer educator role, either before or during the experience. The Leadership Challenge, developed through substantial research with college students in leadership positions, presents five practices of exemplary leadership. Leadership Challenge instructional resources use examples and case studies, which peer educators can easily relate to and are drawn from classroom and cocurricular settings. Students are provided with a self-assessment to assist them in recognizing the exemplary leadership practices in their own lives. They are prompted to reflect on their leadership experiences and note the time(s) when they were at their personal best (Kouzes & Posner, 1998b). The students then reflect on the decisions and behaviors that helped them put forth their best leadership efforts. Trainees can share these with one another and then identify ways to incorporate those same behaviors into their work within the first-year seminar.

In addition to an assessment of the practices where they are most strong, students are provided with a list of ways they can enhance their skills in the behaviors where they may have room for growth. Thus, a student who wants to become better at "modeling the way" may try reaching out to others by challenging himself or herself to "say 'hi' and learn about what [others] are doing" (Kouzes & Posner, 1998a, p. 66). These types of suggestions are clearly applicable to the first-year seminar where it is important to make all students feel included, and a peer will have the opportunity and the responsibility to interact with others.

The Leadership Challenge is adaptable to different training programs. It can be incorporated into one- or two-day sessions as a supplement to the training content, or can serve as the theoretical framework for a more comprehensive training program.

The Peer Leadership Model (PLM) developed by Komives and Adelman (2002) is another useful resource, but it is best suited for an ongoing and concurrent training program when students have the opportunity to consider the leadership practices relevant to their experience. The PLM frames the nature of peer relationships around two dimensions: power and organization. The authors use examples of peer leadership at higher education institutions to demonstrate how leadership occurs based on the influence between peers. For example, the literature on peer involvement suggests that linking new students to peers who are already involved on campus can prompt new students to find involvement opportunities of their own (Komives & Adelman). As such, first-year seminars with the goal of creating meaningful campus engagement among first-year students rely on upper-division peer educators to share involvement opportunities and to orient new students to the many resources offered by the institution. In this way, the first-year seminar is a laboratory of leadership learning, providing many opportunities for peers to practice their leadership skills and recognize their power and influence as it relates to their less-experienced peers. Similarly, using the PLM as a component of peer training provides a framework for students who have already served in the role of peer educator to relate their experiences to an incoming cohort of peers.

Training content should blend theoretical as well as practical strategies. Using teaching techniques that can be applied to the first-year seminar classroom and modeling the appropriate blend of presentation and application of new concepts will help keep peer leaders engaged in the training process. When training participants have an opportunity to not only hear about effective facilitation but also practice the skills being presented, they are more likely to have confidence in applying what they have learned through training to a real interaction with a student.

Training Delivery Models

The most effective way to thoroughly prepare peers for their role in the first-year seminar is to offer ongoing training leading up to and throughout their experience. There are several ways to organize ongoing training opportunities, and the delivery method varies greatly depending on program needs or resources. Some programs use a credit-bearing course to allow peer leaders to gain academic credit for their service. Others use workshops focused on specific content and offered at appropriate times throughout the peer leadership experience. One of the benefits of a long-term training program is the ability to present topics at times when they are most relevant to the peer leaders. For example, if peer leaders are expected to provide support during the fall advisement process, sharing information midsemester, when advisement is approaching, may lead to better engagement from the peer leaders than if this information is presented in a spring training session when advisement is several months away. In an extended training setting, topics can also be expanded on and studied more thoroughly by the peers.

Whatever the method selected, the four-phase model presented earlier can be applied to ongoing training experiences just as easily as to one-time events. In the extended training model, facilitators can spend more time in each phase. For example, in a one-time event, facilitators may have less time to explore the needs of first-year students (Phase 2) because more time is needed for introducing and processing the value of campus resources (Phase 3). Extended training programs allow for greater balance in the topics presented and provide trainees with the opportunity to apply what they are learning to the actual peer leader experience. While it is more resource-intensive to support an ongoing training experience, such an effort has a greater likelihood to lend itself to opportunities for application and reflection—two factors critical to student learning and development.

Peer Leader Training Courses

Hamid and Gardner (2001) recommend the use of credit-bearing courses that "[provide] specific instruction on the peer leader's duties and the rationale supporting them" as well as a "body of knowledge immediately applicable to the role of the peer leader" (p. 99).

Timing of the training course. Courses designed to prepare and support peer educators may be completed prior to the experience in the classroom or concurrent to the first-year seminar experience. Offering a course prior to the peer education experience allows program administrators to identify any potential challenges peers may face and to address those before the peers' interactions with new students. Such a course may also help program coordinators identify students who may not be suitable for the peer educator role before they enter the classroom. Pre-experience courses may help peers feel more prepared and confident because they have had a chance to learn about relevant campus resources and teaching strategies before entering the classroom for the first time. The challenge of offering a course prior to the experience is that peers do not have a frame of reference for the information presented. Facilitators must rely on hypothetical situations through the presentation of case studies or role-playing.

Providing ongoing training through a concurrent course allows the peers to consider and apply information applicable to the peer leadership experience, at the times when it is most relevant. This type of time-released training mirrors the first-year seminar, which is often structured to present information at times when it is most readily applied to the transition cycle and when students are most likely to be engaged. For example, peers who are expected to provide support and instruction about responsible decisions regarding alcohol can be trained on strategies to engage students around this topic as well as the resources that are available to students at the beginning of the semester before first-year students have formed unhealthy habits rather than at the midpoint of the semester when students may have already made uninformed decisions about their alcohol use. Time-sensitive training benefits peer leaders by allowing them to focus on small chunks of content rather than being overwhelmed by the entire range of expectations prior to the leadership experience.

Developing a training course. Peer leadership courses are housed in a variety of academic departments. Options for course homes include the colleges of education or humanities, arts, and sciences; within the academic leadership curriculum; or in student life. Instructors for peer leadership courses should be involved in the administration or teaching of the first-year seminar so they understand the unique role of the peer leader. They should also be knowledgeable about student leadership development. One option is to team teach the training course with an instructor and an experienced peer leader. This partnership allows the instructional team to model appropriate team teaching. Just as peer leaders serve as role models for new students, veteran peer leaders can model appropriate behavior to their peers. This also provides an opportunity for experienced peer leaders to stay involved with the first-year seminar program, with different responsibilities.

In addition, a leadership course provides a vehicle for assessing the impact of the peer leadership experience. For example, course activities can be designed to allow students the opportunity to practice the skills necessary for success in a peer leadership role. Instructors of the leadership course can gauge the needs of the peers based on performance on class activities and assignments. If peers are having trouble grasping a particular concept, the instructor can address that further, as opposed to a one-time training model where only a specified amount of time can be allotted to each content area.

Benefits of training courses. Peer leadership training courses allow program administrators to practice regular supervision of the peer leader staff. Since most of the time required of the peer leader is spent either in the first-year seminar classroom or in one-to-one or small-group mentoring, seminar administrators may not have many opportunities to interact with the peers. A course that meets regularly can help the staff maintain an accurate perspective about program successes and opportunities.

A training course can also serve as a method of compensation by providing academic credit rather than financial remuneration for the peer leadership experience. Using course credit as compensation may aid the peers in viewing the experience as a service, or leadership opportunity, rather than as a job. Peer leadership courses (often upper-level courses) can be a great incentive for students to consider such positions. Program administrators should strive to have a higher course number (300-500 level) assigned and offer two to three units of academic credit to assure students of the value of the training experience. It is also important to advertise the leadership course as a required component of the peer education experience so that students can plan accordingly, reserving space for the course in their academic plan and schedule.

Course curricula. The curricula for training courses vary depending on the type of first-year seminar being offered and the expectations of the peer leadership role. Ideally, the course will provide opportunities for peers to learn more about specific job functions, provide an academic environment where students in this unique role can learn about and develop their mentoring skills, and either prepare for the experience they are about to have as a peer educator, or reflect upon the experience and its impact on others as well as themselves as it is occurring.

Not-for-Credit Ongoing Training

If conducting training through a leadership course is not an option, program administrators should consider other ways to extend the training experience. For example, weekly or biweekly in-service trainings can be an effective way to reach the peer leadership cohort outside of a classroom structure. If peer leaders are expected to attend these types of workshops, this should be indicated in the hiring materials or contract. It may also be helpful to note the consequences of missed workshops. In the absence of course credit, students who are already heavily involved on campus may not have the same commitment to attend as they would if they were receiving a grade for their efforts.

Virtual Training

Students may also be able to share and reflect on experiences through classroom management systems like Blackboard or Angel. Prompting students to contribute to a web-based discussion board or submit reflective journals via electronic format may allow program administrators to stay informed about the students' experiences when face-to-face meetings are not feasible. The use of web-based communities can supplement face-to-face trainings as well. Online systems also allow program administrators to post content, such as important announcements, relevant readings, and accolades for peers' achievements.

Training Resources

First-year seminar programs are often administered by a small number of faculty or staff. As a result, designing a comprehensive training program can seem daunting. Fortunately, there are many resources available to assist program administrators in this task. In addition to the resources presented in this chapter, the bibliography in appendix A provides print and online resources relevant to the development of peer educators. Other resources to consider are key campus partners who may assist in other training and development efforts. For example, centers for teaching excellence or faculty development can offer guidance on training content and methods. Faculty in education often have significant experience and expertise in curriculum design and can be helpful in developing training programs that promote participation and engagement.

Peer educators are used in many areas of campus life—admissions, athletics, academic support programs (e.g., Supplemental Instruction, tutoring, writing center), campus ministry, community service, counseling, judicial affairs, multicultural education, orientation, health services, residence life, student government, and study abroad. Many of the skills peer leaders need to be successful in the first-year seminar are common to other peer educator roles, and since training programs are designed around the expected skills of the participants, there are likely commonalities between departments' training content. As such, first-year seminar administrators can look to the various places on campus where peers are being used and share training resources and strategies with colleagues in those areas. Collaborative work with campus partners allows for idea and resource sharing and provides opportunities to work more strategically to meet program goals. Tapping into campus resources and identifying key partnerships can provide essential support to the training and development of peer leaders.

Conclusion

Training and development is a critical component of a peer leadership program. Effective training programs are grounded in a foundation of learning outcomes that drive the content, processes, and evaluation of the training efforts. Using active-learning strategies and modeling the expectations of the peers in the first-year seminar classroom are key strategies for effective training. Training initiatives should be comprehensive and designed to provide support to peer leaders throughout their experience. While a variety of frameworks exist to serve as the backbone of a training experience, program administrators should create an approach that best suits the needs of their unique peer leadership program.

RECOMMENDED READINGS FOR PEER EDUCATORS
ON FIRST-YEAR STUDENT DEVELOPMENT

Evans, N. J., Forney, D. S., Guido, F. M., Patton, L. D., & Renn, K. A. (2010). *Student development in college: Theory, research and practice*. San Francisco, CA: Jossey-Bass.

» Perry's theory of intellectual and ethical development (pp. 82-98)
» Schlossberg's transition theory (pp. 212-226)

Mullendore, R. H., & Banahan, L. (2007). *Empowering parents of first-year college students: A guide for success*. Columbia, SC: University of South Carolina, National Resource Center for The First-Year Experience and Students in Transition.

Upcraft, M. L., Gardner, J. N., & Barefoot, B.O. (2005). *Challenging and supporting the first-year student*. San Francisco, CA: Jossey-Bass.

Chapter 5
Evaluating the Use of Peer Educators

     The greatest challenge in the assessment of a peer education program is that many audiences are affected by the peer educator role. Thus, evaluation efforts must be diverse and multifaceted to capture the many aspects of the peer-to-peer learning experience. First-year seminar directors likely want to explore the impact of the peer educator program on the students served, the peer educators themselves, and the larger seminar program. In addition to exploring outcomes related to peer education, program administrators will also want to engage in some process-based assessments. Assessment should examine the effectiveness of the peer leader program in achieving its goals with respect to peer leader development, recruitment and selection, and training. Using a variety of methods, administrators can determine the strengths of the peer education program as well as the areas where improvements may be made. This chapter will present strategies for developing a comprehensive assessment process for peer leadership programs associated with first-year seminars.

Impact of the Peer Educator Program on the Students Served

     The motivation for program administrators to implement a peer education component of the first-year seminar likely comes from a desire to enhance the experience of the students enrolled in the course. The effects on the upper-division students serving in the role of peer leadership may be secondary to that initial motivation. Similarly, assessment efforts related to the seminar frequently center on the evaluation of first-year students' learning and development and employ a variety of methods, including course evaluations, student and instructor interviews, institutional data, and locally developed and commercially available survey instruments. Respondents to the 2009 National Survey of First-Year Seminars reported using the National Survey of Student Engagement, the Freshman Survey and its companion Your First College Year, the Community College Survey of Student Engagement, and the First-Year Initiative, among others, to assess outcomes related to the first-year seminar (Padgett & Keup, 2011). There are, however, fewer readily available tools to assess the impact that a peer educator has on student learning in the seminar. A universal instrument would be difficult to develop because of the varied uses and responsibilities of peer leaders within the seminar classroom. Yet, the impact of peer education can be assessed without a unique instrument. Presented here are some strategies that may be used to gauge the contribution peer educators make to seminar outcomes for students served.

End-of-Course Evaluations

Most institutions require enrolled students to evaluate courses at the end of each semester. These evaluations usually include items about instructor effectiveness, such as availability outside of class, efficiency in returning assignments, providing feedback, and so on. Adding a few items about the role of the peer leader can provide valuable feedback about individual performance when results are disaggregated at the section level. In the aggregate, items on the course evaluation may provide insight into the contribution of peer education to the seminar as a whole. Items do not have to be lengthy or complex and may include the following:

- » My peer leader made important contributions to our class.
- » My peer leader was approachable.
- » My peer leader was helpful to me outside of class.
- » My peer leader was an appropriate role model.
- » My peer leader was a valuable part of my first-year seminar experience.

Simple, open-ended prompts that do not add too much length to an existing end-of-course evaluation may also be included instead of, or in addition to, close-ended items. Such prompts allow students to provide more detail regarding their perception of the peer leader. Sample survey items may include

- » Please comment on the role of the peer leader.
- » Please provide any feedback regarding the effectiveness of the peer leader.

Focus Groups

End-of-course evaluations will provide valuable information about the effectiveness of individual peer leaders and a high-level view of the potential contribution they make to the program. Yet, evaluations typically do not allow students to elaborate on what they see as the strengths and challenges of the peer leader role. Focus groups comprised of students from a variety of sections (who then have experiences with a range of peer leaders) can help provide insight into the effectiveness of the program on the whole and capture the breadth of roles peer leaders play in various classrooms. The focus group protocol may include the following prompts:

> » Tell us about your peer leader.
> » Describe your relationship with him or her.
> » What role has he or she played in your first-year seminar experience?

University-Wide Assessments

Given the availability of national survey instruments that measure various outcomes of the first-year experience, there are likely departments on each campus collecting data that can be linked to the peer leadership program. For example, if a survey is distributed to gauge students' satisfaction with their first year, they may be asked to identify a peer or peers who have contributed to their satisfaction. If a peer leader is mentioned in this survey, that can be valuable information for the first-year seminar program. It is often possible to add institution-specific items to standardized survey instruments. For example, program administrators may ask students at the end of their first year, Did you feel that you had a mentor or an experienced peer to whom you could talk? or To whom did you turn when you had questions or concerns? Working collaboratively with campus partners who are conducting assessment in other areas or toward different learning outcomes, can make assessment efforts more manageable.

Impact of the Peer Education Experience on the Peer Educators

Chapter 1 presented several reasons students are attracted to the peer leadership role, and rarely does a student indicate personal gain as part of his or her motivation. Many students have selfless intentions and are drawn to the peer educator role by a desire to help others be successful. Harmon (2006) found that students had no expectations for their own learning when serving as a peer mentor for first-year students. However, serving in such positions can have a significant impact on student learning and development, as seen in chapter 2. Some methods for capturing the outcomes specific to the peer educator are presented here.

Ongoing Reflection

One of the keys to helping peer leaders realize the benefits of their role is to prompt them to reflect on their experiences throughout their service. Reflection activities for peer leaders should allow them the opportunity to (a) consider the impact that their work has had on others and (b) write and speak about the impact this experience has had on themselves. This type of reflection starts with the application process by asking students what skills they will bring to this role and what they are hoping to learn as a result of their participation. Reflection should continue during training with a more formalized goal-setting process where peer leaders are prompted to consider what they hope to gain from this experience and what actions they will take to ensure that they make progress toward those goals.

Ongoing training programs allow program administrators to strategically place reflection opportunities throughout the semester and to collect those reflections and analyze the progress students are making at an individual and program level. Assessment through reflection can be as simple as a one-minute paper prompt: What has been your greatest challenge in the peer leader role so far? What has been your greatest success in the peer leader role so far? Midpoint reflection may direct students to recall their initial motivation for the role or ask them to revisit the goals they set at the beginning of the experience and describe their progress in meeting those goals. They may also be asked to engage in planning for goal achievement for the second half of their experience. End-of-experience reflection can be even more substantial by providing students with an opportunity to synthesize what they learned through training, their interactions with their co-instructor, and their engagement with first-year students. This type of reflection can be powerful for students and will provide program administrators with an in-depth understanding of the experiences of the peer leaders. Appalachian State University employs an end-of-experience evaluation that might also be used to promote this type of reflection (appendix D).

Self-Evaluation

Reflecting on the peer leadership experience allows students to consider the impact it has had upon them. Such reflection may not, however, provide program administrators with a thorough review of the effort that the peer put forth toward the job duties and responsibilities. Self-evaluation can be a helpful means of assessment, as much of the work of peer leaders is done without direct supervision. While a co-instructor can directly observe classroom facilitation, peers often have responsibilities to students that extend beyond the classroom. As such, self-evaluation strategies become an important way to capture information about the peer leader experience and program effectiveness. Program administrators also have the opportunity to compare the peer leaders' perceptions of their service to those of the students served and of the co-instructors. When combined with other assessment strategies, self-evaluation may give some insight into which aspects of the peer leader's performance had the most impact. Moreover, because self-evaluation is an indirect measure of effectiveness and looks at the program through a narrow lens (i.e., the perspectives on an individual peer leader), it is extremely important to triangulate these data with other information collected about the seminar.

The University of Cincinnati uses a comprehensive evaluation at the end of the peer leader service (see appendix D). Students are prompted to evaluate themselves with respect to their practice of key leadership behaviors, which were emphasized in training. Specific questions include

> » In which of the presented leadership behaviors have you, as a peer leader, most improved over the course of your peer leader experience?
> » Considering the role of the peer leader, in what areas do you think you excelled? Where did you have the most difficulty?
> » How and why did you improve in each area?

Student responses are then compared to their pre- and post-assessments in these areas and used as a means of providing feedback to the peer leaders as well as assisting program administrators in identifying areas where improvements can be made.

Instructor's Perspectives of Peer Leader Effectiveness

Coupling a self-evaluation with an evaluation from the co-instructor can give a more comprehensive view of the peer educator's effectiveness. Instructors have a unique perspective on the peer leaders' growth during the experience, as they observe the peers facilitating classroom activities and interacting less formally with the first-year students. This type of evaluation serves a two-fold purpose: (a) to offer peer leaders feedback about their performance and (b) to determine the impact they had on the course and students.

At the University of South Carolina, first-year seminar faculty evaluations of the peer leader account for 30% of the students' final grade in the required peer leadership course. Assigning academic credit to their work with first-year students may make peer educators more accountable for their performance while reinforcing the idea that peer education is a learning experience for them as well as for the students served. A sample of the evaluation that is submitted by the instructors can be found in appendix D.

Impact of the Peer Educator Program on the Success of the First-Year Seminar

Peer education programs contribute to overall first-year seminar success in many ways. Newton and Ender (2010) posit "peer educators are valuable for an academic institution because they are experienced with the campus, they are economical to the budget, they can relate to the situations of fellow students, and they are effective" (p. 3). Yet, in order to justify the resources devoted to their selection, training, and compensation, it is important to be able to measure and articulate these impacts.

Cost-Benefit Analysis

When conducting a cost-analysis of a peer leadership program, administrators should consider training hours, staff dedicated to program support, marketing expenses, and student compensation (e.g., stipends, course credit, or other forms of nonmonetary compensation). These costs can seem significant, but if the benefits to the first-year students and to the peer educators themselves are found to be substantial, these costs are easily justified. Further, if students' enjoy their experience and return for a second or third year of service in the peer leadership role, the value of the time spent training and preparing the student increases exponentially. Veteran peers who demonstrated skill in selected areas can be plugged into more advanced leadership roles, such as, serving as peer leader captains and assisting with recruitment, selection, and training.

To the extent that first-year seminar participation can be linked to student retention and that interaction with peer leaders may contribute to student satisfaction with the course and/or the larger institution, program administrators may also want to factor first-year retention rates into their cost analysis. In other words, if peer leaders contribute to the seminar's power as a retention initiative, then they may have an indirect impact on new student retention. As was noted in chapter 2, participation in peer leadership experiences may also contribute to the peer educator's desire to remain at the institution.

Program Reputation and Marketing

Course reputations are difficult to establish and even more difficult to change. Unfortunately, students and others may sometimes dismiss the first-year seminar as unimportant or as a fluff course (i.e., not college level). In this respect, peer leaders can serve as course ambassadors, sharing the benefits of the course with prospective students and their families and assisting administrators in their efforts to present the course in a positive light. Because first-year students are easily influenced by their peers, they will likely take cues from them with respect to course selection and registration. If a seminar is an optional course, accolades from a peer may influence a student to register. For a required course, the attitude of peer leaders can set the tone for the expectations new students have about the first-year seminar experience. As program administrators look at the overall impact of peer leaders on the first-year seminar, they will want to consider their role in maintaining the reputation of the seminar as a high-quality learning experience.

The impact peers have on program reputation can be difficult to measure, however. To gauge this, students enrolled in the seminar might be interviewed or asked to participate in focus groups related to the formation of course expectations just prior to or during the first week of class. Similarly, questions that provide insight into program reputation and effectiveness of marketing can be included on the course evaluation. Questions that program administrators might ask include, How did you first hear about the seminar? What are your expectations for this course? What do you know about the first-year seminar? Where or how did you form these opinions? and Who influenced your ideas about the course? Such information will provide insight into the potential for peers to influence the reputation of the course and encourage registration for and positive attitudes about the seminar. It may also suggest areas that may need greater attention in the recruitment, selection, and initial training of peer leaders.

Peer Educator Program Evaluation

When evaluating the effectiveness of a peer leader component, administrators will want to understand the outcomes associated with the program. They will also want to know which processes or aspects of the program may have contributed to those outcomes. That is, program coordinators need to identify more specifically the areas of greatest effectiveness as well as the areas where more development is necessary.

Evaluation of Program Goals and Outcomes

While program goals vary based on the purpose and expectations of the peer leaders, some common goals for a first-year seminar peer educator component may include improving student retention (Cuseo, 2010b), increasing student satisfaction and persistence within the first-year seminar, enhancing social integration into the institutional community (Cuseo, 1991; Newton & Ender, 2010), and providing opportunities for student leadership development (Pascarella & Terenzini, 2005). These goals should be clearly articulated to the peer leaders throughout the recruitment, selection, and training processes. Assessment strategies should be selected with the goal in mind. While it may seem most convenient to evaluate goal achievement at the end of the experience, ongoing assessment allows administrators to capture progress throughout and make adjustments as necessary.

Strategies for ongoing assessment may include asking peer leaders to provide a written update (e.g., blog post or reflection paper) about their experiences so far as they might pertain to specific goals. For example, if a goal of the peer leadership program is to develop mentoring, teaching, and communication skills in peer leaders, prompts may ask students to share the ways in which they have practiced those skills in their interactions with the students in the seminar. Asking students to rate the usefulness of training they received on these skills using a Likert-type scale yields quantitative data, which may lend itself to interpretation more easily. Comparing student responses to this type of question at different moments in time might suggest places in the experience where peers are more likely to draw on training resources. Such information could help program coordinators do a better job delivering just-in-time training content. It may also suggest topics from earlier training sessions that require additional time and attention.

These types of assessments can be completed anonymously or with identifiers if the assessments will also be used by peers and program administrators as part of individual performance evaluations. The assessment may occur within a training session or in the absence of concurrent training, using course management or survey distribution software.

Benchmarking allows institutions with similar programs, student populations, missions, or organization to compare the results of their initiatives. This may be more challenging to do with peer leadership programs, however, because the differences between programs are usually vast and the student participants are less homogeneous than students enrolled in the first-year seminar. Yet, some opportunities to compare the experiences of peer leaders to students in similar roles do exist. The University of South Carolina conducts an annual campuswide survey of peer education. Coordinated by the Office of Student Engagement, the survey is distributed to students who serve in a variety of peer education roles, including resident mentors, student health educators, first-year seminar peer leaders, orientation leaders, and ambassadors. Results are collected by this central office and distributed in department-specific as well as aggregate form. This project assists the University in understanding the gains that peer educators are seeing as a result of their experiences. Findings include students' reporting that their peer leadership experience

» Increased their knowledge of University services
» Improved communication skills
» Increased their confidence in leading others in times of academic or personal difficulty
» Increased interaction with faculty
» Involved interacting with diverse groups
» Helped them hold themselves more accountable (University of South Carolina, 2008-2009, p. 2)

Campuswide assessments like this can be informative for first-year seminar administrators in that they allow for the comparison of outcomes with peer programs that may have different goals or purposes. It may also help program coordinators identify potential campus partners who are excelling in areas where the seminar peer educator program may need additional development.

Evaluation of Recruitment and Selection

Because students' needs, preferences, and learning styles are constantly evolving, it is important that recruitment and selection processes be evaluated annually. Results should be used to make improvements prior to the next recruitment cycle to ensure that students continue to show enthusiasm for the peer educator role.

One method for evaluating these processes is to ask the current cohort to consider his or her experiences and share ideas for improvement. Training sessions or development workshops where many peer leaders are present are appropriate for gathering this type of information. Program administrators may want to ask current peer leaders to reflect on recruiting strategies and comment on what worked, what did not work, and what can be done differently. Since many peer leaders serve in multiple roles on campus, they can offer suggestions based on their experiences with other programs. Asking current peer leaders for ideas of how to market the opportunity in a way that it will be seen and understood by perspective peer leaders can provide innovative ideas that will help the first-year seminar peer education role stand out from other leadership and service positions on campus.

Evaluation of Program Training and Development

The greatest amount of time needed to support a peer leadership program is the time spent preparing students for their role. Whether training efforts are one-shot meetings, multiday workshops, or ongoing processes (i.e., semester-long preparation or leadership courses), evaluation of training and development efforts is critical.

Evaluation should take place at two points in time: immediately following a training intervention (e.g., a one-time training event, an individual session in an ongoing training program or course) and after the student has had the opportunity to reflect upon and apply the skills and behaviors that were addressed through the training experience. Simple session evaluations that capture immediate reactions can help administrators identify points of highest engagement and interest from the students. End-of-session evaluations questions might include the following:

> » As a result of this workshop, to what extent do you feel prepared for your role as a peer leader?

» What was the most valuable part of this training session?
» After participating in this training, what additional tools, resources, and/or training do you still need to feel prepared for your role as a peer leader?

Collecting data immediately following the training experience helps program coordinators make adjustments for future presentations of the same training content. It may also highlight areas that need to be a focus of future training efforts. For example, if students report they need further preparation regarding conflict management, program administrators can identify a future opportunity to elaborate on this particular skill.

It is equally important to evaluate the effectiveness of training once students are engaged in the peer educator role. Peer leaders may not recognize the value of some content until they have had the opportunity to apply it. For example, at the end of a spring training event, peers may rank an overview of campus resources as more valuable than a demonstration of active-learning strategies. These same peers may rank active-learning strategies as much more valuable at the end of the experience, suggesting they may not have anticipated the value of this content prior to the opportunity to plan and execute successful lesson plans. Looking at both sets of evaluations would confirm the value of active-learning strategies as a training component while highlighting the need to further explore when peers are exposed to this content.

Conclusion

Whether a peer leadership program is a new component of the first-year seminar or a long-standing tradition, assessment is essential. By gathering information from the many constituents involved in the peer leadership process—first-year students, peer educators, program administrators, campus partners—areas of excellence can be confirmed and celebrated while areas for improvement are identified and addressed. Many peer leader assessment efforts can be easily built into the existing assessment structure for the first-year seminar. The key to determining how the assessment should be conducted is to clearly identify what should be assessed. Clearly developed learning outcomes for the peer leadership program will provide the road map for the assessment journey.

Appendix A
Peer Education Bibliography

Astin, A. W. (1993). *What matters in college: Four critical years revisited.* San Francisco, CA: Jossey-Bass.

Bandura, A. (1986). *Social foundations of thought and action: A social cognitive theory.* Englewood Cliffs, NJ: Prentice-Hall.

Carns, A. W., Carns, M. R., & Wright, J. (1993). Students as paraprofessionals in four-year colleges and universities: Current practice compared to prior practice. *Journal of College Student Development, 34*(5), 388-394.

Chickering, A. W. (1969). Friends, groups, and student culture. In *Education and identity* (pp. 253-279). San Francisco, CA: Jossey-Bass.

Croll, N., Jurs, E., & Kennedy, S. (1993). Total quality assurance and peer education. *Journal of American College Health, 41*(6), 247-249.

Cuseo, J. (2011, October 10). *Peer power: Empirical evidence for the positive impact of peer interaction, support, and leadership.* FYE Listserv post: http://listserv.sc.edu/cgi-bin/wa?A1=ind1110B&L=FYE-LIST

Drellishak, R. (1997). The merits of peer education programs. *Journal of American College Health, 45*(5), 218.

Edelstein, M. E., & Gonyer, P. (1993). Planning for the future of peer education. *Journal of American College Health, 41*(6), 255-257.

Ender, S. C., & Newton, F. B. (2000). *Students helping students: A guide for peer educators on college campuses.* San Francisco, CA: Jossey-Bass.

Engstrom, E. L. (Ed.). (1995). *Enhancing peer education programs.* Baltimore, MD: American College Health Association.

McKeachie, W. J. (1986). *Teaching and learning in the college classroom: A review of the research literature.* Washington, DC: National Center for Research to Improve Postsecondary Teaching and Learning.

Pascarella E. T., & Terenzini, P. T. (1991). *How college affects students: Findings and insights from twenty years of research.* San Francisco, CA: Jossey-Bass.

Pascarella, E. T., & Terenzini, P. T. (2005). *How college affects students: A third decade of research*. San Francisco, CA: Jossey-Bass.

Russel, J. H., & Shinkle, R. R. (1990). Evaluation of peer-adviser effectiveness. *Journal of College Student Development, 31*(5), 388-394.

Terenzini, P. T., Pascarella, E. T., & Blimling, G. S. (1996). Student's out-of-class experiences and their influence on learning and cognitive development: A literature review. *Journal of College Student Development, 37*(2), 149-162.

Appendix B
Building Peer-Instructor Relationships

University of Kentucky
UK 101 Planning Workshop Agenda

1. Check-in and distribution of materials and common reading book
2. Get to know your co-instructor time (questions provided)
3. Welcome
4. Interactive exercise on concerns, anxieties, and excitement of the first-year students—quotes from Lexington high school seniors
5. Core curriculum for all UK 101 sections (go through handout that outlines required topics and assignments)
6. Syllabus
   - » Required reading (common reading book)
   - » Course learning outcomes
   - » Course requirements
   - » Attendance policy
   - » Homework policy
   - » Sample syllabus
7. The instructor-peer instructor partnership (make both aware of each other's roles)
   - » Responsibilities of instructor
   - » Responsibilities of peer instructor
   - » Joint responsibilities
8. Overview of resources on UK 101 website
9. Reminder about future training dates for new instructors (faculty or professional staff) and all peer instructors

10. Work time as teaching team
   » Assign responsibilities
   » Begin planning syllabus

Questions for Getting to Know Your Co-Instructor

» Where are you from?
» How long have you been at UK?
» Why are you teaching UK 101 or UK 201?
» What is your favorite thing about UK?
» What are your plans for the summer?
» How many years have you been teaching UK 101 or UK 201?
» What are your goals for the class?
» How do you prefer to communicate (e.g., e-mail, phone, in person)?
» What is your teaching style?

If you have already taught together in the past, catch up or talk about
» How you will improve your class
» Your favorite class session
» Any class sessions you might want to change

Roles and Resposibilities

Resposibilites	Instructor	Peer Instructor
Attend class	X	X
Develop course syllabus	X	Should have input
Prepare for class	X	X
Make announcements at beginning of each class		X
Take attendance; create and ask attendance questions; enter into spreadsheet		
Send e-mails to students about campus activities and cultural events		X
Lead class discussions		
Read and respond to reflection entries		
Grade assignments (e.g., library, quiz, APEX quiz, common reading paper)	X	Should have input
Enter grades on spreadsheet	X	
Make arrangements for technology as needed		
Maintain Blackboard (optional)		
Make arrangements for guest speakers		
Assign final grade for the semester	X	Should have input
Meet one-on-one with students (optional)		
Integrate the course readings (e.g., common readings) into the class		
Make copies and prepare materials for class		
Correspond with students		
Has the final say on class issues and decisions	X	

Building Your UK 101 or UK 102 Syllabus

Class Section	Topic	Instructor	Peer Instructor
1	First Class	X	X
2			
3			
4			
5			
6			
7			
8			
9			
10			
11			
12			
13			
14			
15			
16			
17			
18			
19			
20			
21	Last Class	X	X

Appendix C
Training Models

University of South Carolina

The University of South Carolina provides training and development for peer leaders in the first-year seminar through two major processes: (a) a one-day preliminary training in the spring semester and (b) a course taken concurrently with service in the first-year seminar classroom.

Following the selection of the fall cohort, peer leaders participate in a one-day training session, which offers a big picture overview of the roles and responsibilities of the peer leader as well as the expectations from the first-year seminar program. The learning outcomes of this session include

» Understanding the purpose, goals, and success of UNIV 101
» Understanding the role, expectations, and commitments of a University 101 peer leader as it pertains to students, faculty, and the curriculum
» Being able to articulate his or her desired role and responsibilities in UNIV 101
» Developing tools and ideas for specific course content and activities
» Exploring ways to deal with the challenges a University 101 peer leader may experience

A sample agenda for this one-day training event is listed below.

One-Day Training Agenda

10:00 am	Gathering and check-in
10:30 am	Welcome
	History, philosophy, and success of University 101 Programs
11:00 am	Community building
11:45 am	Understanding first-year students
12:00 pm	Lunch
	Panel of former instructors and peer leaders
1:30 pm	Active-learning strategies
2:30 pm	Sticky situations
3:30 pm	Wrap-up and evaluation

Through a partnership with the College of Education at the University of South Carolina, the University 101 program offers a three-credit course (EDLP 520) for students serving in the role of peer leader for the first-year seminar. Students are required to enroll in the EDLP 520 course during the semester in which they are serving in the first-year seminar classroom. This weekly session allows the peers to discuss issues as they encounter them in their peer leadership role. It also provides a regular opportunity for the program staff to offer training and development on a variety of topics aimed at preparing the peers for their classroom role as well as developing their leadership skills. The value of receiving course credit for their service as a peer leader enhances the experience and builds in accountability. The grade for the EDLP 520 course is determined by an evaluation from the first-year seminar instructor (30%) and the evaluation of work submitted for the EDLP 520 course (70%). A sample syllabus follows.

EDLP 520: Peer Leader Training and Leadership Course Syllabus

Purpose

You have been selected to participate in a leadership program that focuses on helping first-year students succeed at the University of South Carolina. Your academic success, personal involvement, leadership, and commitment to university service make you a model of successful student behavior. Your willingness to work closely with a University 101 instructor to encourage student success is reflective of the caring spirit that characterizes this institution. Our seminar will focus not only on helping you be an important support person in your University 101 class but also on developing leadership and communication skills that will be useful in other settings.

Course Description

EDLP 520 is a unique class designed to provide a forum for the evaluation, reflection, and processing of your experiences as a University 101 peer leader. Discussion will revolve around such topics as fostering student learning, classroom management techniques, helping skills, and effective communication. It might be useful for you to consider the approximately 40 contact hours in your University 101 class as a lab or practicum, with the class meetings of EDLP 520 as a discussion or lecture class.

Learning Outcomes

As a result of this course, students will

- » Articulate the personal development resulting from the peer leader experience
- » Apply knowledge of first-year students and engaging pedagogies to the development and delivery of an effective lesson plan for use in University 101
- » Develop and apply appropriate transferable skills, such as communication, helping, and leadership skills
- » Develop and share ideas for specific course activities or discussions
- » Identify strategies to deal with challenges associated with the peer leader role

Selected Weekly Course Topics

- » Facilitating discussion regarding alcohol and drugs
- » First-year reflections and student development theory
- » Strategies for community building
- » Creating effective lesson plans
- » Engaging and active-learning strategies
- » Assisting first-year students in the advising process
- » Helping skills
- » Appreciating diverse perspectives
- » Leadership development
- » Marketing the peer leadership experience

Descriptions of Selected Assignments and Projects

Instructor Interview and Goal Setting

It is important that you form a positive relationship with your University 101 co-instructor. The key to strong teaching partnerships is regular communication. Additionally, you should have a clear understanding of each of your roles and responsibilities to the class as well as the expectations that you have of each other. To help you strengthen the partnership between you and your co-instructor, you will interview your co-instructor for your first assignment. Using the questions provided as a guide (you do not have to use only these questions; you may add others) and the goal-setting sheet that you started in the peer leader training workshop, you should spend 45 minutes to an hour talking with your co-instructor about your expectations and goals for the semester. Following this interview, you will submit a two- to three-page summary of your time together. This paper should include, but is not limited to, your reactions to your interview, what most excites you about the peer leader experience with your University 101 class, the expectations you set for yourselves and for the students in your class, any concerns you still have, and your plan for regular communication throughout the semester.

Peer Leader Journal

Throughout the semester you will complete five journal entries. These journal entries are meant to be a way for you to reflect freely on the peer leader experience. Some possible topics are (a) the challenges and successes you are having in building community, (b) your role as a mentor and as a leader for your students, (c) your relationship with your co-instructor, (d) successful activities you have facilitated in class, and (e) the impact you believe it has had on your students and on what we have read or discussed in EDLP 520.

Model Lesson Plan

It is expected that you will share in the teaching responsibilities of your University 101 course. Following our class discussion about teaching strategies, you will have the opportunity to practice your teaching skills. Each of you will create a lesson plan that is to be used in your University 101 class. Topics will be chosen during class. Resources will be provided to assist with the development of this model class outline.

Student Interviews

You will meet individually with three students in your University 101 class to find out how they are adjusting to college life. Interview guidelines will be provided. Each student will submit a written description of his or her student interviews, each student's progress in adjusting to college, and your reactions to your students' needs. You should relate any findings from your interviews to relevant EDLP discussions and readings (e.g., student development theory, teaching strategies, learning styles).

Appendix D
Assessing Peer Leadership

Peer Leader Evaluation
Appalachian State University

Your work in Freshman Seminar this year has helped shape the college experience for some 1,400 new students. You have added to the University's rich heritage of caring about students. Your work, viewed from the many angles of student evaluations, faculty reports, and outcomes assessment, demonstrates that your commitment mattered in the lives and success of the 2006 freshman class. We sincerely appreciate what you have done this semester.

Although you have given so much already, we are asking that you make yet another contribution to Freshman Seminar. An honest and thorough evaluation of your experiences as a peer leader is needed to pave the way for improvements next year. Please complete this survey to help us learn from our mistakes and build on our successes.

Role in freshman seminar class	Strongly agree				Strongly disagree
I frequently talk to some students in my section outside of class time.	5	4	3	2	1
I had an open dialogue with my instructor about my role in the class and/or course plans.	5	4	3	2	1
I met with my Freshman Seminar instructor before the syllabus was completed.	5	4	3	2	1
I often met with the instructor outside of class for planning.	5	4	3	2	1
I had a daily duty such as taking attendance, leading an activity, etc.	5	4	3	2	1

Satisfication	Strongly agree				Strongly disagree
The experience of being a peer leader was worthwhile.	5	4	3	2	1
If I had it to do over, I would make the decision to be a peer leader.	5	4	3	2	1
My advice and feedback were valued in planning for the class.	5	4	3	2	1
I enjoyed the relationship with my instructor.	5	4	3	2	1
I believe I have made a difference in my students' lives.	5	4	3	2	1
I was satisfied with my role in the Freshman Seminar classroom.	5	4	3	2	1
	Very much				Not at all
How time-consuming were your duties in Freshman Seminar?	5	4	3	2	1
Peer leader seminar/experience	Strongly agree				Strongly disagree
Seminar class time was well spent.	5	4	3	2	1
Having a former peer leader as a co-instructor was valuable.	5	4	3	2	1
The instructors encouraged meaningful class discussions.	5	4	3	2	1
I often met with the instructor outside of class for planning.	5	4	3	2	1
The instructors provided sufficient opportunities for questions.	5	4	3	2	1
The amount of work required was reasonable.	5	4	3	2	1
The following topics discussed in class were helpful:					
» Alcohol discusion	5	4	3	2	1
» Teaching class/effective presentations	5	4	3	2	1
» Helping skills	5	4	3	2	1
» Marketing the peer leader experience	5	4	3	2	1

	Strongly agree				Strongly disagree
I learned things in Peer Leader Seminar that I applied to my Freshman Seminar class.	5	4	3	2	1
I learned things in Peer Leader Seminar that will be useful in other settings.	5	4	3	2	1
I felt I had a place or person to go to if I experienced difficulties with any aspect of my role as a peer leader.	5	4	3	2	1
Peer Leader Seminar is a necessary corequisite to being a peer leader.	5	4	3	2	1
I would have become a peer leader even without academic credit (thus no Peer Leader Seminar).	5	4	3	2	1
As a result of this course and experience, I have strengthened my					
» Interpersonal communication skills	5	4	3	2	1
» Presentation and facilitation skills	5	4	3	2	1
» Helping skills	5	4	3	2	1
» Leadership skills	5	4	3	2	1
The training session in the spring was useful.	5	4	3	2	1
Demographics	Yes	No			
Did you take Freshman Seminar?					
Did you know your FS instructor before this semester?					
Did you attend the training session this spring?					
Did you attend some or all of the New Directions conference in August?					

1. What information or strategies discussed in Peer Leader Seminar did you use or apply in your Freshman Seminar class?

2. What aspects of your peer leader experience as a whole will you apply to other settings?

3. Please share any suggestions you have for improving the Peer Leader Seminar below or on the back of this sheet.

Peer Leader Self-Evaluation
University of Cincinnati

(Selected Items from Peer Leader Evaluation, Winter 2012)

Self-Rating Items

Using a scale of 1 (not at all effective) to 5 (extremely effective), rate yourself on each of the following peer leader capacities:

- » Generating student buy-in in learning community
- » Enhancing group bonding within the learning community
- » Planning high-quality learning community meetings
- » Facilitating learning community meetings
- » Communicating to learning community via Blackboard and e-mail
- » Involving students in the learning community planning process
- » Acquiring and responding to student feedback on learning community
- » Implementing the learning community foundations
- » Involving faculty in learning community
- » Connecting students to advisors
- » Connecting students to campus resources and opportunities
- » Establishing individual relationships with students
- » Mentoring
- » Discussing sensitive issues with students, such as drinking, stress, relationships, and insecurity
- » Integrating diversity activities into the learning community
- » Modeling effective learning habits and strategies
- » Facilitating study groups
- » Facilitating student reflection on academic performance
- » Impacting students' academic development
- » Consistently following through on PL meetings, weekly reports, attendance sheets, office hours, and other PL responsibilities

Open-Ended Reflection Items

Reflect on your further development during Winter 2012 in the various peer leader roles—that is, team leader, mentor, learning coach, connector, coworker, or otherwise.

1. What are you most proud of and why?

2. What have been your most significant challenges, and how have you handled them?

3. In what areas would you like to develop further, and how you might do so?

4. How has being a peer leader affected you?

Instructor Evaluation of Peer Leader
University of South Carolina

Thank you for working with an undergraduate peer leader this semester. Your support and mentorship of the peer leaders is a critical component of the peer leader program. In an effort to assess the effectiveness of the peers who serve as co-instructors and to determine your satisfaction with your teaching partnership, we request that all instructors who work with a peer submit a final evaluation as a component of EDLP 520: The Teacher as Manager, the required course for all first-time University 101 peer leaders. This evaluation will count toward 30% of your peer leader's grade in this class. We do recommend that you go over this evaluation with your peer leader so that he or she receives feedback about the performance directly from you.

Name of Peer Leader:	
Instructor:	

For each area below, check the description that best fits your judgment of your peer leader. Please also share this evaluation with your peer leader.

	Outstanding	Good	Needs improvement	Not acceptable
ATTITUDE: Was the peer leader (PL) enthusiastic, diligent, interested and courteous? Comments:	☐	☐	☐	☐
APPROACHABILITY: Did students appear to find the PL approachable in and out of class? Comments:	☐	☐	☐	☐
COOPERATION: Did the PL work effectively with others? Was she or he tactful when dealing with students or visitors? Comments:	☐	☐	☐	☐
RESPONSIBILITY: Was the PL reliable in performing work assignments and carrying out instructions? Comments:	☐	☐	☐	☐

EFFECTIVENESS:
Was the work that the PL performed
valuable and of high quality? Were
presentations organized and effective?
Comments:

ATTENDANCE:
Was the PL faithful in reporting to
class and meetings as scheduled in
a timely manner?
Comments:

ROLE MODEL:
Was the PL an appropriate role model
for new students? Did he or she act
with integrity?
Comments:

IMPACT ON CLASS:
Did the PL have a positive impact on
the class? Did he or she make
meaningful contributions?
Comments:

General Comments: (please feel free to submit an attached letter)

Please indicate whether you would recommend this student to serve as a peer leader in
the future.
 Recommend
 Recommend with reservations
 Do not recommend

Instructor Signature: _____ Date: _____

References

Adelman, A. L. (2002). *Peer leadership*. (Leadership Insights and Applications Series No. 12). College Park, MD: National Clearinghouse for Leadership Programs.

Antonio, A. (2004). The influence of friendship groups on intellectual self-confidence and educational aspirations in college. *The Journal of Higher Education*, 75(4), 446-471.

Astin, A. W. (1993). *What matters in college: Four critical years revisited*. San Francisco, CA: Jossey-Bass.

Astin, A.W. (1999). Student involvement: A developmental theory for higher education. *Journal of College Student Development*, 40(5), 518-529.

Badura, A. S., Millard, M., Johnson, C., Stewart, A., & Bartolomei, S. (2003). *Positive outcomes of volunteering as a peer mentor: A qualitative study*. (Educational Document Reproduction Services No. ED 473 226)

Baker, S., & Pomerantz, N. (2000). Impact of learning communities on retention at a metropolitan university. *Journal of College Student Retention*, 2(2), 115-126.

Barefoot, B. O. (2002). *Second National Survey of First-Year Academic Practices*. Brevard, NC: Policy Center on the First Year of College. Retrieved http://www.jngi.org/2002nationalsurvey

Black, K. A., & Voelker, J. C. (2008). The role of preceptors in first-year student engagement in introductory courses. *Journal of The First-Year Experience & Students in Transition*, 20(2), 25-44.

Buote, V. (2006). *"If I wasn't friends with these people, I probably wouldn't have adjusted too well:" Friendship development and university adjustment among first-year university students* (Master thesis). Wilfred Laurier University, Waterloo, Ontario.

Chickering, A. W. (1969). *Education and identity*. San Francisco, CA: Jossey-Bass.

Chickering, A. W., & Reisser, L. (1993). *Education and identity* (2nd ed.). San Francisco, CA: Jossey-Bass.

Coleman, J. S. (1961). *The adolescent society*. New York, NY: Free Press.

Colvin, J. W., & Ashman, M. (2010). Roles, risks, and benefits of peer mentoring relationships in higher education. *Mentoring & Tutoring: Partnership in Learning, 18*(2), 121-134.

Cuseo, J. B. (1991). *The freshman orientation seminar: A research-based rationale for its value, delivery, and content.* (Monograph No. 4) Columbia, SC: University of South Carolina, National Resource Center for The Freshman Year Experience.

Cuseo, J. B. (2010a). Peer leadership: Definition, description, and classification. *E-Source for College Transitions, 7*(5), 3-5.

Cuseo, J. B. (2010b). Peer leadership: Situation-specific support roles. *E-Source for College Transitions, 7*(6), 4-5.

Ender, S. C., & Newton, F. B. (2000). *Student helping students: A guide for peer educators on college campuses.* San Francisco, CA: Jossey-Bass.

Feldman, K., & Newcomb, T. M. (1969). *The impact of college on students.* San Francisco, CA: Jossey-Bass.

Gardner, J. N. (1981). Developing faculty as facilitators and mentors. In V. A. Harren, M. H. Daniels, & J. N. Buch (Eds.), *Facilitating students' career development* (New Directions for Student Services No. 14, pp. 67-80). San Francisco, CA: Jossey-Bass.

Griffin, A. M., & Romm, J. (Eds.). (2008). *Exploring the evidence, vol. IV: Reporting research on first-year seminars.* Columbia, SC: University of South Carolina, National Resource Center for The First-Year Experience and Students in Transition. Retrieved from http://www.sc.edu/fye/resources/fyr/index.html

Hamid, S. L. (Ed.) (2001). *Peer leadership: A primer on program essentials* (Monograph No. 32). Columbia, SC: University of South Carolina, National Resource Center for The First-Year Experience and Students in Transition.

Hamid, S. L., & Gardner, J. N. (2001). Summary and recommendations. In S. L. Hamid (Ed.), *Peer leadership: A primer on program essentials* (Monograph No. 32, pp. 97-102). Columbia, SC: University of South Carolina, National Resource Center for The First-Year Experience and Students in Transition.

Harmon, B. V. (2006). A qualitative study of the learning processes and outcomes associated with students who serve as peer mentors. *Journal of The First-Year Experience & Students in Transition, 18*(2), 53-82.

The Hazen Foundation. (1968). *The student in higher education: Report of the committee on the student in higher education.* New Haven, CT: Author.

Hunter, M. S., & Heath, M. M. (2001). The building blocks of the peer leader program: Recruitment, selection, and training. In S. L. Hamid (Ed.), *Peer leadership: A primer on program essentials* (Monograph No. 32, pp. 37-52). Columbia, SC: University of South Carolina, National Resource Center for The First-Year Experience and Students in Transition.

Hunter, M. S., & Linder, C. W. (2005). Faculty development and the first year. In M. L. Upcraft, J. N. Gardner, & B. O. Barefoot (Eds.), *Challenging and supporting the first-year student* (pp. 275-292). San Francisco, CA: Jossey-Bass.

Ishler, J. L., & Upcraft, M. L. (2005). The keys to first-year student persistence. In M. L. Upcraft, J. N. Gardner, & B. O. Barefoot (Eds.), *Challenging and supporting the first-year student* (pp. 27-46). San Francisco, CA: Jossey-Bass.

Keup, J. R., & Skipper, T. L. (2010, March). *Findings from the 2009 National Survey of Peer Leaders*. Presentation at the ACPA Annual Convention, Boston, MA.

Kevesdy, K. M., & Burich, T. A. (1997). *Creating dynamic teaching teams in schools.* Milwaukee, WI: ASQC Quality Press.

Kim, E. (2009). Navigating college life: The role of peer networks in first-year college adaption experience of minority immigrant students. *Journal of The First-Year Experience & Students in Transition, 21*(2), 9-34.

Komives, S. R., & Adelman, A. L. (2002). *The peer leadership model.* Unpublished manuscript.

Kouzes, J., & Posner, B. (1998a). *An instructor's guide to the leadership challenge.* San Francisco, CA: Jossey-Bass.

Kouzes, J., & Posner, B. (1998b). *Student leadership practices inventory: Student workbook.* San Francisco, CA: Jossey-Bass.

Kouzes, J., & Posner, B. (2002). *The leadership challenge* (3rd ed.). San Francisco, CA: Jossey-Bass.

Kouzes, J., & Posner, B. (2007). *The leadership challenge* (4th ed.). San Francisco, CA: Jossey-Bass.

Kuh, G. D., Kinzie, J., Schuh, J. H., Whitt, E. J., & Associates. (2005). *Student success in college.* San Francisco, CA: Jossey-Bass.

Landrum, R. E., & Nelson, L. R. (2002). The undergraduate research assistantship: An analysis of the benefits. *Teaching of Psychology, 29*(1), 15-19.

Larose, S., & Boivin, M. (1998). Attachment of parents, social support expectations, and socioemotional adjustment during the high school-college transition. *Journal of Research on Adolescence, 8*(1), 1–27.

Latino, J. A. (2007). *First-year student ratings of their college environment based on background characteristics* (Unpublished doctoral dissertation). Florida State University, Tallahassee.

Lewis, S. E., & Lewis, J. E. (2005). Departing from lectures: An evaluation of peer-led guided inquiry alternative. *Journal of Chemical Education, 82*(1), 135-140.

Maslow, A. H. (1954). *Motivation and personality.* New York, NY: Harper.

McDill, E. L., & Rigsby, L. C. (1973). *Structure and process in secondary schools: The academic impact of educational climates.* Baltimore, MD: Johns Hopkins University Press.

McKinney, J. S., & Reynolds, P. J. (2002). *Rising from the ashes: The effects of the peer experience in the Phoenix Program* (Unpublished manuscript). Indiana University. Retrieved from http://www.indiana.edu/~educy520/sec5982/week_15/pauline.pdf

National Association of Career Educators (NACE). (2011). *Job outlook 2011.* Retrieved from: http://www.naceweb.org/Home.aspx

National Resource Center for The First-Year Experience and Students in Transition. (2009). *Peer Leadership Survey* [Raw survey data]. Columbia, SC: University of South Carolina, Author.

Newton, F. B., & Ender, S. C. (2010). *Students helping students: A guide for peer educators on college campuses* (2nd ed.). San Francisco, CA: Jossey-Bass.

Padgett, R. D., & Keup, J. R. (2011). *2009 National Survey of First-Year Seminars: Ongoing efforts to support students in transition* (Research Reports on College Transitions No. 2). Columbia, SC: University of South Carolina, National Resource Center for The First-Year Experience and Students in Transition.

Pascarella, E. T., & Terenzini, P. T. (1991). *How college affects students: Findings and insights from twenty years of research.* San Francisco, CA: Jossey-Bass.

Pascarella, E. T., & Terenzini, P. T. (2005). *How college affects students: A third decade of research.* San Francisco, CA: Jossey-Bass.

Paul, E., & Brier, S. (2001). Friendsickness in the transition to college: Precollege predictors and college adjustment correlates. *Journal of Counseling & Development, 79*(1), 77–89.

Reid, E. S. (2008). Mentoring peer mentors: Mentor education and support in the composition program. *Composition Studies, 36*(2), 51-79.

Rice, M., & Brown, R. D. (1990). Developmental factors associated with self-perceptions of mentoring competence and mentoring needs. *Journal of College Student Development, 31*, 293-299.

Rose, G. L. (2003). Enhancement of mentor selection using the ideal mentor scale. *Research in Higher Education, 44*(4), 473-494.

Rosenthal, K. I., & Shinebarger, S. H. (2010, March-April). Peer mentors: Helping bridge the advising gap. *About Campus, 15*(1), 24-27.

Sanft, M., Jensen, M., & McMurray, E. (2008). *Peer mentor companion.* Boston, MA: Houghton Mifflin Company.

Schlossberg, N. K., Waters, E. B., & Goodman, J. (1995). *Counseling adults in transition* (2nd ed.). New York, NY: Springer.

Schrodt, P., Cawyer, C. S., & Sanders, R. (2003). An examination of academic mentoring behaviors and new faculty members' satisfaction with socialization and tenure and promotion processes. *Communication Education, 52*(1), 17-29.

Smith, J. S., & Wertlieb, E. C. (2005). Do first-year college students' expectations align with their first-year experiences? *NASPA Journal, 42*(2), 153-174.

Smith, W. L., & Zhang, P. (2010). The impact of key factors on the transition from high school to college among first-and second-generation students. *Journal of The First-Year Experience & Students in Transition, 22*(2), 49-70.

Stone, M. E., & Jacobs, G. (Eds.). (2008). *Supplemental instruction: Improving first-year student success in high-risk courses* (Monograph No. 7, 3rd ed.). Columbia, SC: University of South Carolina, National Resource Center for The First-Year Experience and Students in Transition.

Swenson, L. M., Nordstrom, A., & Hiester, M. (2008). The role of peer relationships in adjustment to college. *Journal of College Student Development, 49*(6), 551-567.

Switzer, A. M., & Thomas, C. (1998). Implementation, utilization, and outcomes of a minority freshman peer-mentor program at a predominantly White university. *Journal of The Freshman Year Experience & Students in Transition, 10*(1), 31-50.

Terenzini, P. T., Pascarella, E. T., & Blimling, G. S. (1996). Student's out-of-class experiences and their influence on learning and cognitive development: A literature review. *Journal of College Student Development, 37*(2), 149-162.

Tinto, V. (1993). *Leaving college: Rethinking the causes and cures of student attrition* (2nd ed.). Chicago, IL: The University of Chicago Press.

Tinto, V., & Pusser, B. (2006). *Moving from theory to action: Building a model of institutional action for student success.* Washington, DC: National Postsecondary Education Cooperative.

University of South Carolina, Office of Student Engagement. (2008-2009). *Peer Leadership Survey.* [Executive Summary] Retrieved from: http://www.housing.sc.edu/studentengagement/pl_assessment.html

Upcraft, M. L., & Gardner, J. N. (1989). A comprehensive approach to enhancing freshman success. In M. L. Upcraft, J. N. Gardner, & Associates (Eds.), *The freshman year experience* (pp. 1-12). San Francisco, CA: Jossey-Bass.

Wasburn, M. H. (2008). One mentor or two: An instrumental case study of strategic collaboration and peer mentoring. *Journal of The First-Year Experience & Students in Transition, 20*(2), 91-110.

Weissberg, N., Owen, D., Jenkins, A., & Harburg, E. (2003). The incremental variance problem: Enhancing the predictability of academic success in an urban, commuter institution. *Genetic, Social, and General Psychology Monographs, 129*(2), 153–180.

Wellman, D. A. (2008). *Campus tour guide motivation: The role of intrinsic need satisfaction and autonomy support* (Unpublished doctoral dissertation). University of South Carolina, Columbia.

Wyckoff, S. C. (1999). The academic advising process in higher education: History, research, and improvement. *Recruitment & Retention in Higher Education, 13*(1), 1-3.

Yazedjian, A., Purswell, K. E., Toews, M. L., & Sevin, T. (2007). Adjusting to the first year of college: Students' perceptions of the importance of parental, peer, and institutional support. *Journal of The First-Year Experience & Students in Transition, 19*(2), 29-46.

Index

About the Authors

Jennifer A. Latino is the director of the First-Year Experience at Campbell University. She has served in support roles for transitioning students at a diverse array of institution types, including a private women's college, a community college, large research universities, and a faith-based institution. Through positions in the first-year seminar, first-year experience, new student orientation, student leadership development, and residence life, Latino has developed a thorough understanding of the needs and challenges that face students in transition. Her research interests include identifying and implementing best practices in the first-year seminar, the effective use and support of peer educators, and faculty development. Formerly the associate director for University 101 Programs at the University of South Carolina, Latino is a regularly invited presenter for institutes and conferences sponsored by the National Resource Center for The First-Year Experience and Students in Transition. She earned a bachelor of science degree from the University of North Carolina at Pembroke, a master of science in higher education from North Carolina State University, and a doctorate of education in higher education from Florida State University.

Michelle L. Ashcraft is the assistant director of the Office of New Student and Parent Programs and coordinator of the Common Reading Experience at the University of Kentucky. Her passion for first-year experience work and student leadership development has been cultivated through experience with various transition programs at several large research universities. Through work in new student orientation, first-year experience, peer mentorship, student leadership development, the first-year seminar, and parent programs, Ashcraft has acquired first-hand knowledge of the needs and challenges of both first-year students and peer educators. Her professional interests include enhancing student success and retention, developing student leaders, and building effective peer-mentor programs. Formerly a graduate assistant for University 101 Programs at the University of South Carolina, she uses her experience with the peer- leader program and research sponsored by National Resource Center for The First-Year

Experience and Students in Transition to inform her daily interactions and work with both students in transition and peer educators. Ashcraft earned a bachelor of science degree in organizational leadership and supervision from Purdue University and a master of education degree in higher education and student affairs from the University of South Carolina.